10/3

The Working Mom On The Run Manual

(A.K.A. What The Heck Happened To My Life?)

DEBBIE NIGRO

A MasterMedia Book
New York

Copyright © 1995, Debbie Nigro

Published by MasterMedia Limited.

MASTERMEDIA and colophon are trademarks of MasterMedia Limited.

Library of Congress Cataloging-in-Publication Data

Nigro, Debbie.

   The working mom on the run manual : a.k.a what the heck happened to my life? / Debbie Nigro.
      p. cm.
   ISBN 1-57101-011-4 (alk. paper)
   1. Working mothers—Life skills guides. 2. Mothers—Time management.   I. Title.
HQ759.48.N54   1995
646.7'0085'2—dc20

                                                  95-22716
                                                   CIP

Designed by Teresa M. Carboni and Jennifer McNamara
Printed in the United States of America
Production services by Graafiset, New York

10 9 8 7 6 5 4 3 2

CONTENTS

ACKNOWLEDGMENTS

I'm dedicating this book to Jeff, my partner in life, love and business. In fact, he is the reason I'm able to have a book to write at all. Synergistic talents is how I describe our existence together—two incredibly determined and hard-working people with dreams bigger than most. Day and night, Jeff creates opportunities for me to shine as me—thank you, I love you!

I also dedicate this book to Alexis, my beautiful daughter, without whom I would not be a mother—which is the greatest thing that ever happened to me. I don't even remember changing a diaper before she was born, and was totally annoyed that she came without instructions. They say a mother just knows, and with Alexis, I found out it's true. A beautiful kid—blue eyes, light brown hair, athletic, independent, and has weathered a tumultuous separation and divorce like a champ. She's led a very unconventional kid life—though I'm not quite sure what conventional is anymore, gives me tons of material for the radio show, surprises me, challenges me, and loves me completely unconditionally.

And to Eileen Byrne, a very special young lady—bright, talented, happy, sharp, incredibly hard working, responsible, creative, and mature beyond her years. She's my right hand.

And to all the wonderful baby-sitters who made it possible for me to go to work and practice my craft and make a living without having to worry about the well-being of my daughter.

Gratitude beyond words goes to my Mom, Eileen

Nigro, who has never failed me, even under the most dire circumstances. You gave me some pretty good genes, Ma—thanks!

And to Claire, Jeff's Mom, another incredible lady—who'll drive two hours from Pennsylvania on the dime if you need her.

Then there's Aunt Mary, whom I can't say enough about because she's the absolute best.

And Goldie and Pearl, too, Aunt Mary's neighbors, who treat Aunt Mary like a queen—driving her to pick up Alexis at a moment's notice. And Aunt Eleanor, another favorite, and Aunt Yolie, Aunt Linda and my sister in-law Susie—I'm very lucky to have all of you!

Thanks goes to Louie—Alexis' Dad, and his new wife Doreen and their daughter, Daniella, for keeping life in our blended family pleasant.

And though I have much to say about each of the people that follow, but very little room to say it in, I want to give special thanks and acknowledgment: ZiZi (Italian for auntie), Noreen, Gail DeRaffele, Vicki, Merle, Ralph, Gus, Pat, Judsen Culbreth, Elisa Fershtadt, Ruth Sarfety, Vermel Cayne, and Marge Lovero, who introduced me to the lovely women executives at Avon—who have turned out to be the most incredible support system a person could have.

These Avon women, the executives of a hugely successful company that stands behind everything women care about, took a chance on this local girl with a big idea, and I will be forever grateful. A little timing, a little luck, a little talent, a good idea and a great company and off we went. What began as a local radio show on two stations has, with Avon's support, grown to more than 100 stations and counting throughout the country. Many thanks to my now dear friends Delia deLisser, Nancy Glaser, Gail Blanke, Carolyn Aishton and all my other friends at Avon.

Another very special thanks goes to Susan Stautberg, the lovely and very bright publisher of MasterMedia Limited, who thought enough of me to include me in her repertoire of dreamers who get the chance to publish a book.

Also thanks goes to my editors, Jennifer McNamara and Fredda Pearlson.

And last, but not least, I thank my father John Nigro, for a very special gift he left behind for me–his entrepreneurial spirit

INTRODUCTION

Hi, I'm Debbie Nigro, and for all practical purposes, I'm an intelligent adult. However, I bounce checks (not intentionally, of course!), get parking tickets (and forget to pay them), want to pull my daughter's hair sometimes (and feel really badly after the feeling subsides), wish I was thinner (what else is new?), own mostly black clothes (to look slimmer), try to look younger (it's getting tougher), love and hate men (sometimes in the same day, hour, minute, breath), work like a maniac, and dye my hair once a day.

Sum it up! Get to the point! Gotta Run! That's my life and I imagine it's yours too if you're a busy working Mom. We'd love to be up on everything going on in the world but we're too busy working like maniacs at our jobs, the laundry, garbage, shopping, car pooling, emergency car runs, etc., which take up our energy and attention spans. And this Mom thing is the same kind of life regardless of where you live, how many kids you have, how much money you make, or what nationality you are—it crosses all lines.

Look, I'm no expert, who has the time to be an expert? But in the course of my life I've come across a whole lot of information, especially in the last few years since I started my radio show, "The Working Mom on the Run, a.k.a. What the Heck Happened to My Life?" where I champion the cause of working Moms everywhere. My show airs live out of New York every Saturday from 10 a.m. to noon and is picked up on 113 stations throughout the country. Sponsored by Avon Products, you can call (212) 546-7118 to find out where it airs in your area.

As a group, we Moms are incredibly smart and resourceful, while at the same time, we're totally out of our minds! We really can't do everything perfectly, but we'll never admit it! We'll try until we die to make it all right for everybody every day. But no one's handing out plaques, which is a shame because I kinda like plaques.... Oh, and we do complain! But in case you haven't noticed, nobody cares! For a few minutes you'll get an ear, but then it's just you again ... sometimes feeling a little sorry for yourself ... but not for long because there's always something else to do!

Get to the point! Okay! This book is meant to help simplify your life a bit. It's filled with information you can't really file anywhere and if you could, or did, you probably wouldn't be able to find it when you need it. So here it is, all in one neat little place.

But it's hard to believe I'm the one giving advice here—especially since I barely had time to write this book! Let me give you a little peek at what it was like taking on the mammoth project. A book? Me? ... NO PROBLEM!

I'd been meaning to write a book for a long time. Every day I'd walk around with all these notes I'd jotted down—great ideas. I'd tell myself I'd do it on the train— begin writing my book, that is—but then the only seat left was between a couple with six suitcases. And on those rare occasions when I'd actually have seat of my own and not be sandwiched in between other commuters, suddenly I'd remember that I'd forgot to do my nails ... so I'd try polishing them without spilling my coffee all over the newspaper that's squeezed between my arm and rib cage ... and then I'd remember I still have to put on my make-up! So then I'd say to myself I'll do it in the taxi—at least jot down some more notes—so I'd try that, but the Pakistani driver—who just arrived in this country yesterday—is going 90 miles an hour and he doesn't even know where he's going! And who could concentrate when he keeps turning around and asking me a million questions—causing my adrenaline to shoot through the top of my head while I'm praying he doesn't hit the bus that's pulling up on the right.

I could work on it at the office, I'd say, if the phones would stop ringing and if I could ever get caught up on god-knows-how many backed up voice-mail messages.... But first I have to call the baby-sitter and tell her my mother will be picking up my daughter today ... or was I suppose to call my mother to tell her I can't pick her up...? Well, I have to tell the baby-sitter something, but I can't reach her so I'd better call the school secretary so she can relay the message to my daughter. But who is going to baby-sit tomorrow when I have to leave for Boston at 6 a.m.? Oh well, maybe I'll work on the book at lunch—but first I have to clear off a space on my desk to write....

Maybe after lunch, no—no time then, I have to go to the gym to meet—get this, my personal trainer!— who's trying to get me in shape to do an exercise video that I've committed myself to doing in two weeks—the same two weeks that just happen to fall within the span of the three weeks I have left to get this book to my publisher! Oh, and I can't think about eating bread (because of the video), which makes me want it even more, and when I get back from the gym I have a meeting. And, I'm in major sweat trying to get my pantyhose back on in a room filled with steam...

I'd write the book on the way home from work but I'm carrying too much stuff and I can't figure out which one of the bags has the notes I wrote while I was in line at the bank. Besides, I have to eat the pasta salad I bought for dinner because I'm starving and it'll probably be after seven by the time I get home and the baby-sitter will have already fed my daughter ... and I don't want to waste time eating when I'm home because that will cut into the quality time I can spend with my daughter before she has to go to bed.

My feet are killing me—I can't be creative now! And I just remembered I don't have anything in the house for my daughter's lunch tomorrow—or breakfast—so I'll have to stop by the mini-store at the gas station and pick up some juice packs, bread, milk and cereal for the morning.... Quality time with my daughter is important but it usually turns into me talking incessantly about doing this and not doing that and take your bath and where's your homework and no, you can't have another pudding and the television is too loud and you shouldn't be watching television anyway because it's past your bedtime. And no, there aren't any monsters under the bed, I promise.

Okay, she's in bed and Jeff, my guy, wants me to come sit with him on the couch, but I have to put the stuff away in the kitchen and rinse the stuff in the sink, throw in a load of laundry or two or three, clean up the mess left over from the morning, check the checking accounts and pray that some of the checks I wrote didn't go through before the other checks cleared.... And then, there's still the school notes I have to go through, tests to sign, filling donation envelopes for the PTA's latest fund-raiser ... and then the phone rings and it's my aunt who I meant to call to thank for the money she sent to my daughter ... and she hasn't been feeling well ... and talking reminds me that I'd better call the sitter about tomorrow and then it dawns on me that the only clean pantyhose I have are nude and the dress I want to wear is black ... and all I really want to do is get some sleep! So I wash some pantyhose and leave them hanging and they get really long but who has the energy to rinse and wring them out a million times? I know you're not suppose to put them in the dryer but there's really no choice....

Now, I think, I should work on the book a little but then I think of Jeff who's sitting over there all alone and I haven't even hugged him all day. So I sit down next to him and in five minutes he's snoring and I'm annoyed because when the hell are we supposed to be romantic? Before you know it, I'm right behind him sleeping on the recliner with my neck getting stiff and before I know it, it's one o'clock in the morning and we're trying to pry ourselves off the couch and turn off the lights, lock all the doors and get under the covers but the heat is on too high so I get up, turn it down, I'm thirsty, get some water, the alarm goes off and here we go again ... and I'm definitely going to write that book today!

Well, here's my book—I did it!—and I'd like to dedicate it to the mothers of America. Mothers who, like me, run around each and every day with a million things on their minds—things they have to be on top of or their world and a lot other people's worlds collapse. The Mothers who love their kids, their husbands, their significant others, their families, who love being women and the self-esteem that comes from being productive and effective in and outside of the home. If you're a woman and you're reading this book, you'll understand everything that I just said and everything I'm about to say.

1

Girl
Stuff

*"You show me a woman who hasn't
fantasized getting in a car and leaving
home and I'll show you a woman who
doesn't drive."*

–SUSAN SUSSMAN, NOVELIST

Great quote, the problem is where the hell do you
go? Oh, to be a girl again.... Looking back, what
did we do with all our free time? Sometimes we
really lose it over this one, at least I do.

Take, for instance, waking up in the morning. It used
to be all you had to worry about was your hair—before it
starting turning gray, of course. Now it's a whole new
ball game. There's the initial desire to hide under the
covers and prolong the last precious moment of solitude
before the games begin: first the house mess—the breakfast, the lunches, the list of things to do, whose going
where and needs what and how are they getting there

and back again, what's the money situation and who needs cash, whose clothes are going to the cleaners and what about the fact that you're out of milk and where the hell are you going to write the out-of-milk-thing down so that you actually remember it on the way home—and where is a pen that writes—and what about dinner and on and on.

Next it's facing the music in the bathroom—yes, that same face that needs all these new things to look right (I'll try anything!): cover-ups and blushes and liners and lipsticks and line creams and moisturizers and mousses and gels and gosh, there's a lot of stuff in that cabinet and, aren't you really sick of the whole process by now?

The highlight of the morning is knowing my hair is clean enough to make it through another day—which makes the day seems like a "mini-holiday." Then there's the what-fits routine, which occurs simultaneously with the what-do-I-feel-like-wearing routine, and the search for clean pantyhose with no runs and shoes that don't kill my feet. All that to be followed by the final crescendo: How much stuff can I actually stuff in my pocketbook so it doesn't break my shoulder, and why am I always carrying so much stuff anyway? (Oh, yeah, in case I have to leave the country unexpectedly!)

Then comes "why is the gas tank almost empty," and who the hell has time to stop for gas now, and why does everybody else seem so together? They're not. In fact, they think YOU ARE! What a joke.

Anyway, the girl stuff gets put way back on the back burner once you become the bread-winning household executive called Mom.

*"Zest is the secret of all beauty. There is no
beauty that is attractive without zest."*

-CHRISTIAN DIOR

Zest? Let's start with hair. Why? Because my hair rules
my life, it always has. In fact, the status of my hair has
become inextricably woven with my emotions. Good hair
day, good mood. Bad hair day, bad mood.

It's out of my control. It's the one area of my life around
which I'll never mature. My hair is the worst. Naturally curly
is an understatement. If you took a Brillo pad and unrav-
eled it, you'd know what I'm talking about. If I'm exposed
to humidity, even for a minute, I look like a wild maniac.

My mother and grandmother were both hairdressers,
so I at least learned how to help myself. Helping myself
with my hair meant ironing it on the ironing board (missing is very painful), wrapping it in a tight circle around
my head and securing it every inch of the way with silver
clips, pulling it up on top of my head and rolling the
remainder around a beer can (pathetic), and I've even
tried professionally straightening it with stuff that smelled
like formaldehyde—and it still wasn't straight!

Finally, I figured it out. With a hand-held blow dryer
and brush attachment, I confuse my hair without giving
it a chance to undermine me by blowing it into sections
and securing each piece with a regular small roller—it's
such stupid hair. It cools around the shape of the curler
and when the whole head is done, it pretends it's regular
hair—for a while, that is.

My hair means no beach dates, no pool parties, no
rainy nights on-the-town for me. I'd rather not go

through the public humiliation of turning into Brillo head right before your eyes.

I never even dated a guy if he didn't have air conditioning in his car. For all of you with straight hair, I hate you!

HAIR MYTHS

✓ **When growing out a hairstyle, don't bother with a haircut until you've reached the desired length!**

(Just because you are ready for a new look, there's no reason to stop caring about the one you have now. Trim your hair every 10 to 12 weeks to keep layers from looking scraggly and unkempt— you can't feel pretty with messy hair, and you'll tend to ignore the rest of your beauty routine.)

✓ **Long hair drags your face down and makes you look older.**

(For generations women have been told that long hair will drag down and age an otherwise attractive face. But nowadays every well-trained hair stylist knows that carefully placed angles and layers can do wonders for a face—including hiding a chin and neck that may give away your true age.

✓ **When hair goes gray, go blonde.**

(Unless you were born blonde, chances are going blonde now will drain color from your face and make you appear tired, older and even haggard. Instead of dying your hair blonde, opt for warm brown shades with a hint of red—an instant fix for a drab complexion. Better yet, brighten your new gray hair with a rinse or shampoo formulated to make it sparkle. *Good Houskeeping* magazine.)

Deb's Hair Tips

Best conditioner:
Infusium
Best hair dye:
Castings
Another favorite:
Clairol's Loving Care Color Mousse
Best hair spray:
Style & Hold Spritz-It

THE BEAUTY SALON

Most working Moms are much too busy for beauty salons, but inevitably find themselves there on occasion. If you're getting your hair colored, maximize the experience by getting your nails done at the same time (if you can stand sitting next to women who don't have their heads wrapped in plastic, that is).

Your List:

Dates of past haircuts: _____

_____

_____

Salon: _____

Hairdresser: _____

Location: _____

Phone: _____

Shade and brand name of your color:

_____

(In case your hairdresser leaves the country!)

BEAUTY

How many ancient supplies are you carrying around in your make-up case? Here are couple of facts you should be aware of:

✓ Liquid foundation lasts up to two years, or until it begins to separate.

✓ Toss out face powder and eye shadow after three years or if they turn dry and cakey.

✓ Lipstick is okay for three years, but discard if oil beads up on the sides.

✓ Because mascara and liquid eye-liners are prime breeding ground for bacteria, discard them every three months (*Family Circle*).

Deb Mascara Tip:
I once read that Elizabeth Taylor used
to buy a new mascara and leave it open
overnight to dry a little so it
wouldn't go on too thin. (It works!)

Your List

Names of all brands and shades of make-up items that you finally decided you love (after spending a small fortune on mistakes):

_____

_____

_____

_____

_____

_____

_____

Date you purchased your last mascara so you know when to toss it out:

_____

_____

Brand & date purchased:

_____

_____

LIPS

Why I always have lipstick on my chin after taking a bite of a sandwich is beyond me. Coffee cups are a different story—at least you always know which mug is yours. But, why I'd rather give up kissing than wearing lipstick is another story altogether.

Deb's Lip Tip:

Avon's Perfect Wear Lipstick—looks gorgeous all day and comes in 10 shades. Won't feather or bleed and has vitamin E. Call **1-800-FOR-AVON**.

Here are some great tips straight from the lips of Avon's International Beauty and Fashion Director Kathleen Walas, author of *Real Beauty ... Real Women*:

✓ Make lips look fuller by smoothing gloss over a light or bright lipstick.

✓ Line lips with pencil that matches your lipstick or is a hint darker, but the line shouldn't be obvious.

✓ For a shiny look, rub a little mineral oil or a dab of petroleum jelly over lips before applying color.

✓ For a super natural semi-matte look that really stays put, gloss over with a little petroleum or a lip pencil in an earthy tone.

✓ To make teeth look whiter, use cool lip colors in clear blue-reds, rose and burgundy. Avoid yellow-based colors like orange, brown, cinnamon, peach and apricot.

✓ To keep lipstick from sticking when you're lips are cold, cup your hands over your mouth for a few seconds and warm them in your breath so lipstick will go on smoothly.

Your List:

List the exact names of shades and brands of your favorite lipsticks in the event they get lost or worn off the lipstick case—if it's your favorite, it will!) And if it's my favorite, you can bet they'll discontinue it.

Shade & brand _____

Shade & brand _____

Shade & brand _____

Shade & brand _____

Shade & brand _____

Shade & brand _____

EYE TIPS

DEB*servation:* Eye yi yi, it's really happening! I'm getting older ... as if I need this extra aggravation. I almost slammed into a Mack truck trying to pull back the skin around my eyes in my rear view mirror! What's a girl to do? (Start saving that loose change for the surgery to shore up that loose skin, that's what!)

Next to your lips, the most delicate part of your face is

the skin around your eyes. Starting in your teens and twenties, you should start wearing sunglasses to protect your skin from the sun. Be sure to buy sunglasses with good quality lenses that screen out ultra violet rays.

When you reach your late twenties or early thirties, you may notice the beginning of a few fine lines at the corners of your eyes—this is when you begin to panic. You can prevent "crows feet" by using an eye gel or cream containing a sunscreen. If crows feet are already apparent, a moisturizing gel will make the skin a little plumper, which will make skin look smoother and cause the lines to disappear a bit.

A nightly moisturizing cream is a must. Choose a rich eye cream if your skin is dry, a lighter one if your skin is oily or even just normal. Rub the cream onto the brow bones and eye lids around the corners of eyes, and also under the eyes.

Don't glop the cream on, too much can result in puffy eyes. Don't rub the cream in too hard either, as you can stretch and damage this delicate area.

DARK CIRCLES

DEB_servation:_ Yup, count me in for this one. But I've found something for it that I really love—cover cream concealers. Besides making dark circles far less noticeable, concealers even our skin tone, cover and neutralize other ugly skin discolorations and blemishes. Physician's Formula concealers contain chemical-free sunscreens and come in five shades—yellow to correct blue-based skin discolorations, such as dark circles; green to correct red discolorations; and ice green to correct lightly reddened skin discolorations. Call 800-227-0333 to find where the line of concealers is sold.

NAILS

Deb Fun Fact: I invited a bunch of working Mom friends of mine to a lunch to help me decide if I was on track about what this book should be. I was embarrassed because my nails looked awful, so I announced my flaw and, all at once, they all hid their hands beneath the table cloth—ha! The point is, most working Moms don't have the time to have their nails done professionally—at least not consistently.

If I had the time, I have my nails done all the time—I can never quite do them as good myself. In fact, I have the worst time keeping up with these little suckers. I somehow always leave them till last, and have, on a number of occasions, found myself polishing my nails while racing to get somewhere at 70 miles an hour. I've polished on the train, in my office—you name it. After completing the polishing ritual—no matter in what odd spot or circumstance I may be—I somehow inevitably manage to reach into a pocket or purse (mine, of course) and wreck one!

When this happens to you, and I'm sure it does, dab on polish remover with a cotton ball held by the knuckles of your index and middle fingers and then redo it. If you have just a tiny smudge on one nail, use the pad of your index finger and dab a hint of remover over smudged area with a super light touch. Let it dry and then apply a coat of enamel.

The manicure isn't really the problem, it's the necessary drying time that you can't seem to spare. Here's an idea: Try doing just a few steps at one sitting—which also helps you avoid rushing through it and not doing as nice a job. Do your first coat at night, the next in the morning, and sometime later in the day do another. Nails turn out much better if each coat has time to dry before putting on the next.

To repair tiny cracks, buff your nails, which also makes them shiny and smooth. The best method is to apply oil containing vitamin E, then gently going over them with a buffer.

The best way to protect your nails after all your effort is to apply a top coat to give them a hard finish.

A great overnight treatment for cuticles is globbing on petroleum jelly and covering your hands with a pair of cotton gloves. Your skin will absorb the condensed moisturizer, which will make your nails flexible and healthy (*McCall's*).

Your List

Write down the name of the polish you spent 20 minutes picking out at the nail salon so you don't go through this again the next time!

Shade for nails
_____

_____

Shade for toes
_____

_____

FACE CREAM

Oh, there's that face in the mirror again! And I'm examining it a lot more these days and a lot more closely.

Believe it or not, I use Avon's "anti-aging" cream, Anew, every day—and my mother actually remarked how much my skin had changed (mother's notice everything, you know). I always had problem skin, and at 37, I'm forced to give the age thing a little attention, so I tried it. Though skeptical at first, I was amazed that it actually changed my skin.

Anew works because it contains alpha-hydroxy acids, which transform the appearance of your skin by loosening the bonds holding dead surface skin together and preventing the build-up of the dead skin on the skin's surface. With continued use, Anew improves the appearance of skin by diminishing the visibility of fine dry lines and wrinkles, while giving it a glowing, more radiant, appearance.

A TAN FOR ALL SEASONS

It's a shame the sun is bad for you! I'm happiest when I'm frying on the beach like a rump roast. Fear of ending up looking like a leather purse has led me to self-tanners.

Self-tanning lotions are great in all seasons. They pick up tired-looking winter skin, as well save summer skin from the aging, leathery look the sun gives it.

After you use it, wait an hour before you put on your clothes or shower. (This naked hour wandering period confuses me!) Also, wash your hands with a wash cloth immediately after you apply it. My favorite brand is Estee Lauder's Super Tan.

DEB*tip:*
For really great looking skin, drink as much
water as you can stand.

FRAGRANCES

"What's that lovely fragrance you're wearing? Oh, yeah? I've got to get that!" Yeah, sure I'll get it, as soon as I remember to get it—sometime in the year 2005—or as soon as I have any extra cash that's not already promised for paper towels and orange juice, or which ever comes first!

Anyway, when it comes to perfumes and colognes, try and have more than one, says *Good Houskeeping* magazine. If you wear the same one every day your brain numbs out to the smell, making it easy to apply too much without realizing it. (a string of people choking as you pass them might indicate that you've overdone it!). Also, apply scents to your skin, not your clothes; and wear strong scents in cold weather since cold air diminishes a fragrance's impact. In the summer it's best to wear light scents since the chemistry off warm air has the opposite effect.

List the names of all the perfumes you've smelled and loved and that you'll never remember if you don't write them down here:

_____

_____

_____

List the names of perfumes your friends and relatives use so the next time you want to buy them something special, you'll know:

_____

_____

_____

_____

_____

CLOTHES, CLOTHES, CLOTHES

Do you have sliding scale wardrobe? A closet filled with clothes that used to fit, clothes that do fit and clothes that never fit but you refuse to get rid of anyway in case they do fit someday? Me, too!

As far as wearing what's in my wardrobe, I've evolved as somewhat of an expert in the art of camouflage—using every possible angle to look five pounds thinner, even though I'm usually 10 pounds heavier than I want to be.

For the sake of fashion, I wear undergarments that cut off my circulation. Push-up bras are terrific, too—so what if I can't see over the steering wheel, it's worth it. And even though I'm sick of black, more black clothes seem to find their way into my wardrobe. I wear shoulder pads with everything, even though the fashion moguls say they're out! (Did you ever see what they think is in?)

DEB*tips:*

✓ Don't wear clothes that you don't feel great in! Comfortable clothes make all the difference in how your day goes.

✓ Don't give a darn about what's in or out—wear what you love. Style is what you make your own.

✓ L'eggs Sheer Energy pantyhose really give you an edge—they suck in your legs and hips and they are a must under slacks!

✓ Don't rule out consignment shops. They are great fun, and places where you can find the most amazing stuff. You'd be surprised who drops stuff off and who stops in to pick it up.

✓ Don't get taken to the cleaners! When the dry cleaner gives you a blouse or shirt back with a different stain on it, a missing button or if it is irreversibly damaged, ask the proprietor for compensation.

✓ To avoid unwanted—and untimely!—stains, don't apply makeup, perfume, deodorant or hair spray for at least five minutes before you get dressed.

✓ Clothes packed too tightly in the washer

rub together and cause pilling. Zip zippers and snap snaps to keep things from catching and ruining other items.

✓ Wear a scarf to keep makeup, moisture and dirt off your collar.

✓ Keys and other heavy objects in pockets cause linings to wear thin.

✓ Put jewelry on after you dress to avoid snags.

SHOPPING

I get incredibly excited when I go shopping and find something on the 50 percent-off rack that I actually like, and then see the clerk take another 20 percent off at the register. But inevitably, instead of keeping my mouth shut, I tell anyone I run into while I'm wearing it the whole story of how it was on sale—50 percent la la la—and how it ended up costing me 50 cents or something! Instead of impressing people thinking I'm so "chi chi," they just think I'm cheap cheap!

THIS AND THAT

There's a women's clothes rental company in Boston called Changes where, for $99 a month (plus dry cleaning), women can choose what to wear each day from among a $360,000 wardrobe of business attire. For more information, call 617-723-2299.

Shopping expert Elysa Lazar says some clothing outlets stock merchandise made just for them—clothes you can't

...nd in department stores, while some outlets only carry overflow from their stores. Ralph Lauren, J. Crew and Giorgio Armani are among the latter. Many outlets also carry "irregulars"—merchandise with slight imperfections that is marked down considerably.

A great resource for outlet shopping is Elysa Lazar's *The Outlet Shopper's Guide,* which includes a comprehensive list of outlet stores across the United States, Canada and the Virgin Islands. Available in major bookstores, or by calling 212-982-9300.

MAIL ORDER

Ninety million American consumers spend about $30 billion a year shopping by mail. *Shop by Mail* is a good guide to what's available through the post, listing more than 1,000 of the best mail order companies from which you can buy anything from caviar to cowboy boots. To order a copy, call (212) 982-9300.

FASHION EMERGENCIES

When little fashion emergencies occur, here are some really handy hints (*McCall's*):

✓ Hair spray stops a run in your panty hose dead in its tracks. Spray the top and bottom of the run and let dry 30 seconds.

✓ Zipper that rips? Take a large (two-inch) safety pin and with the head on the inside of the dress weave the pin in and out of the fabric a few times. It works even better with a friend to hold the two sides of the zipper together.

✓ Fix a broken heel by removing the shoe and applying several drops of instant glue between the heel and the shoe. Slip the shoe back on and put pressure on with your foot until the heel holds.

MATCHMAKER, MATCHMAKER

Here's something we all need—clothes and accessories to fill in our wardrobe. You may actually start to enjoy wearing some of the things you have if you take some time to go through your closet and write down all the great things you own that you need to add something to in order to make an outfit. It could be a matching shirt, a belt, a scarf, certain earrings, special pantyhose or under-wear, socks, etc. If you write them down and glance at this book it'll remind you and maybe you'll actually fol-low through one of these days!

Example: have blue slacks need a vest

Have: _____

    Need: _____

Have: _____

    Need: _____

Have: _____

    Need: _____

Have: _____

    Need: _____

Have: _____

    Need: _____

TWO ESSENTIALS

✓ Buy camisoles and tank tops in every color—you always need them to go under suits, blazers, etc. (otherwise, you never have the right color when you need it!)

✓ Begin and keep a list of stores you passed that you loved that you had no time to go in, but that you want to remember to go back to someday when you actually have a free moment—jot down the name of store, the location and what they sell.

Your List

Store/location _____

Sells _____

Store/location _____

Sells _____

Store/location _____

Sells _____

Store/location _____

Sells _____

DEB*servation:*

✓ High heels raise the angle of the butt and give the illusion of thinness.

✓ High heels were obviously invented by a man ... no woman would do this to another woman!

WHAT A HEEL

Finally! Rose-Lee Shoes of Beverly Hills offers us the interchangeable heel. These shoes feature a patented heel screw device engineered at the base of the sole that allows a woman to adapt her heel height and style to both mood and purpose; heights range from one-to-three inches, and it takes only 10 seconds to change a heel!

Women can choose from among seven styles that are available in eight colors of suede and leather—including shades ranging from au courant spice colors such as earthy cayenne to brilliant jewel tones such as navy. The entire line is priced from $60. For more information, call 800-444-HEELS or 310-289-3095.

DEB*tip:*

Easy Spirit shoes are a great comfort choice, so are most suede shoes.

FITTING IN FITNESS

I've considered hosting the first high-heeled marathon ... instead I directed my attention to a much more realistic endeavor: "The Working Mom on the Run Anytime/Anywhere Workout." No kidding! I just recently finished this—see the back page for how to get a copy of the video.

I really wanted to call this "The Who's Kidding Who Exercise Video"—but word was I might not be taken seriously, and this is a serious topic. Every day it's the same scenario ... wake up, vow that this is the day, start off with a low fat food itinerary and swear to start to exercise! Then ... it's always something! right? And, before you know it, it's the next morning and you're playing the same head games with yourself. Meanwhile you're starting to feel worse and worse about yourself—and worse yet because you're losing the pleats in your pants!

So, like you, I was getting aggravated and decided to figure this out.

I enlisted the help of professionals—a kinesiologist and a personal trainer—and created the solution to every busy woman's dilemma: wanting to exercise but not having the time, money or the energy.

My solution: Weave the exercise throughout your day, wherever you are, whatever you do, because there isn't going a to be a block of free time every day (or any day, for that matter) to dedicate to this. THIS is reality.

An example of an anytime/anwhere exercise, which I demonstrate in my video, is push-ups at the bathroom sink. Before starting the exercise, remove all rugs or anything else that could cause you to slip. Also, put a towel over the edge of the sink so you don't hurt your hands. Now you are ready to begin:

Place your feet shoulder width apart, and place your hands on the edge of the sink (or counter) slightly wider than shoulder width. Make sure your feet are far enough back so that when you begin the exercise, your body is in a straight line.

While keeping your body straight and your head in a neutral position, slowly lower your body toward the edge of the sink or counter—aiming it at the center of your chest. As you push back up, exhale. Be careful not to lock your arms. For best results, do three sets of eight to 15 repetitions.

DEB*news:*

Research has found that you don't have to exercise a half-an-hour all at once to get good fitness results ... short bouts of exercise interspersed throughout the day work just as well!
The Center for Disease Control and Prevention and American College of Sports Medicine have found that exercise can be done in short spurts ... eight minutes here, 10 minutes there, for a total calorie expenditure of 200 calories a day (*USA Today*).

So, you bet your tail I'm doing those push-ups on the sink every morning, and leg lifts on line at the bank, and

I'm bicep curling my big black bag, and squeezing the book between my knees for inner thigh tightening while I'm on the phone at the office.

All these exercises and more are in the video. It really works. I actually got back into shape (I was way out) by practicing the exercises to get in decent enough shape to do the video—which I still can't believe I did!

DEB*tip:*

Buy a really big bottle of water and keep it near you all day, sipping until all the water's gone. You'll be in the bathroom a couple of extra times but you'll feel great. Water does wonders for everything and actually helps you lose weight.

EXERCISE AND HEALTH

Women who walk a mile a day whether on a track or in the course of a busy day, reduce their chances of losing bone density as they age. A study by Dr. Elizabeth Krall of the Agricultural Research Service, focusing on walking as a specific type of exercise, found that walkers have up to seven years worth more bone in reserve than non-walkers. "A major finding of the study was that the type of walking that women were already doing in their day-to-day routines is probably benefiting their bones and doesn't require any major change in their exercise habits" (*Wall Street Journal*).

Your List

Exercises to remember—name the body part and the exercise you just read about somewhere and write it down here:

Body part   **Exercise**

_____

_____

_____

_____

_____

When exercising, always remember to:

✓ Consult a physician before beginning any exercise program.

✓ If you feel any light-headedness, dizziness or nausea, discontinue the workout.

✓ Always warm-up and stretch first.

✓ Seek the advice of a fitness professional to help design an exercise program personally tailored for you.

✓ Remember the four basic components of any exercise program are:

1. Cardiovascular/aerobic training
2. Strength training
3. Flexibility
4. Diet ... yes, diet!

✓ Always drink at least six ounces of cold water every 15 minutes during exercise. Why cold water? Because it is absorbed into the system faster.

✓ Consistency is everything. Even the most moderate program done everyday will yield results over time.

✓ Your workouts should be a pyramid. Start off by doing moderate exercise and work up to strenuous activity. Try to exercise three to four times a week (Frank Dow and Donovan Goodreau, One 2 One Personal Fitness, New York City).

2

Women & Men Things

I'm still under the ridiculous impression that Saturday night is date night. Not that I actually ever go anywhere, but I pretend I will. I think about who I can call to baby-sit, what I should wear, and where Jeff and I should go. As the work week grinds on and I get closer to the weekend, I'm exhausted, and the thought of trying on clothes that don't fit, spending money that's already spoken for, and spending even more time away from my daughter turns me off to the idea of going out altogether. Besides, I haven't done my nails, the weather's rotten, I'm having a bad hair week, and the idea of spending Saturday night on the couch—with a pizza or some really good Chinese food—and waking up early and refreshed on Sunday doesn't sound so bad.

For you who are content and don't have to agonize as

much over the Saturday night thing—or for those of you whose agony comes in a different package—I'm sure you've discovered by now that having a good marriage isn't just luck.

A good marriage is a creative process that gets more challenging when it's combined with parenting. Children naturally benefit when parents have a good marriage. A good marriage requires cultivating essential qualities, such as intimacy, trust and communication—the building blocks of a loving partnership. A few good practices include:

✓ Making time for your spouse. Child and job demands take their toll, as well as do anger, frustration, disappointment and other underlying feelings of which you might not be aware.

✓ Be vigilant about giving attention to your marriage. Talk about your individual needs for intimacy, how much time you would each like to spend together and other life needs.

✓ Be creative about finding one-on-one time. For instance, you and your spouse might have coffee together each night after the kids are asleep, or breakfast each morning after the kids are off to school. When it's not possible for you to have daily time together, make ritual weekend plans such as going to the movies on Saturday night or having Sunday brunch (*Child* magazine).

✓ When trying to resolve intimacy problems, take personality types into consideration. If you're married to a workaholic, for example, remind him of what he's missing instead of nagging him about not spending enough time at home. Also take a look at yourself to see if you may be out-of-step in the intimacy dance!

✓ Be clever about solutions to time pressures. Ask what home tasks can be delegated to each other, other caregivers and the kids. Often in our desire to do it all, we take away precious couple time. Some grandparents are just waiting to be asked to baby-sit. Or having a neighbor watch your child, and reciprocating, is another good way to gain some breathing time for your relationship (*Child* magazine).

✓ If you are dieting (and who isn't?), don't over-do it. Extreme dieters often feel hungry, cranky and edgy, which can stifle sexual desire.

Warning signs that your lover is bored:

1. Passionless kisses
2. Frequent sighing
3. Moved, left no forwarding address (Matt Groening)

FUELING THE FIRE

According to America's sexiest wives, based on a survey conducted by *Ladies' Home Journal,* women today are more honest and adventurous in the bedroom than ever before. Highly sensual wives reported making love more often and with greater skill than other respondents. Their secrets?

✓ Be affectionate. Let your husband know how much he is loved, cook his favorite foods, call him during the day to tell him you love him, and write love notes. Husbands reciprocate with romantic gestures of their own.

Every couple can benefit from this kind of nurturing says Evelyn Mochetta, D.S.W., a marriage counselor in New York City. "Sex begins outside the bedroom," she says.

✓ Try a little spontaneity. Sexy wives break the rules. They seduce their husbands when the urge strikes.

✓ Be adventurous. Getting out of the bedroom is one of the ways married couples can be more innovative. Instead of safe sex behind a locked bedroom door, enjoy making love in unexpected places.

According to an article in *Family Circle*, there are five ways to nurture love:

1. Have a sexual fantasy about your husband (oh yes you can!).

2. Say something nice about him to someone—and make sure he over hears you!

3. Surprise him with a kiss. Not the usual peck, but a real on-the-lips, I-love-you kiss.

4. Buy him a surprise gift, something he really wants, not something you think he should want.

5. Reminisce together about the things you did when it was easy to be in love.

AFFORDABLE ROMANCE

When funds are low but the to urge for romance is high, there are many ways to fan the fire and still stay within your means. Celebrate a special occasion by going out to lunch instead of dinner—everything will be the same except for the check, which is usually about half the price. Also, look for early bird specials and beat the crowd.

Two-for-one specials advertised in newspapers and coupon books are also good for staying within a budget, but watch out for appetizers and drinks—they add to the bill quickly.

Happy Hours at bars that serve hot and cold hors d'oeuvres are a good way to have a little time out with your spouse for the cost of a half-price drink or soda and a tip. Sometimes it's nice to get dressed-up and go out for dessert—cheesecake and coffee for two will probably cost less than $15 (Patricia Gallagher's *Raising Happy Kids on a Reasonable Budget*).

TURN-OFFS

There are a lot of things that can take the romance out of a marriage or relationship, particularly anger over who does the chores. Women who work the triple shift—an outside job, child care giving and housework—would rather collapse than make love at the end of a long day. And if they can't count on a man to at least doing his share around the house, some nasty feelings will fester until the idea of having sex holds as much appeal as having a root canal.

When a man is a burden instead of a helpmate, his partner begins to see him as one of the children, and nothing will dry up sexual desire faster than feeling like you are your husband's mother.

DIVORCE

> *"When I meet a man I ask myself, is this the man I want my children to spend their weekends with?"*
>
> —RITA RUDNER

Okay, you've tried everything and you're convinced it's not right any more. If you find yourself in this unfortunate—but all too common—circumstance, there are things that you'll find discover on your own, and other things you need to know from the outset.

The following checklist of do's and don'ts may be helpful if you are preparing for or considering a divorce:

✓ Keep as many records of family finances as possible, including copies of income tax returns, bank statements, rent or mortgage payments, all bills, medical, dental, insurance and pension plans, child care expenses, cost of food, transportation and education, mortgage applications, loan documents, and so on.

✓ Don't use an attorney or accountant recommended by your spouse or by your spouse's attorney or accountant. Divorce is an adversarial proceeding, and not a hint of bias should undermine your case.

✓ Hire an accountant or appraiser to do "discovery" of your spouse's assets. If you can't prove the existence of an asset, you won't be able to share it.

✓ Show proof that you deserve a fair share of an asset. Perhaps you are a wife who assisted your doctor-husband with his practice—working as his nurse, keeping his appointments or books, etc. Or you may have helped your writer-husband with research, typing manuscripts, or editing. You may have made mortgage payments or helped renovate or redecorate your summer house with your own or your parents' money. Be sure to collect receipts and records or keep a diary of your activities.

✓ Don't leave the marital residence. This is probably where the old saw "possession is nine-tenths of the law" originated. Sit it out if you can because once you leave your home, it becomes much tougher to defend your right to future occupancy.

✓ Take your children with you if you leave the marital residence, particularly if you are a woman. It will be very difficult to gain custody if you are perceived as a mother who abandoned her children.

✓ Don't comingle your separate assets. If you deposit your inheritance, gift money, or revenues from your business that existed prior to the marriage into joint bank accounts, it becomes impossible to prove it is your money. It will be considered marital property and subject to division upon divorce. If you owned a home or apartment before marriage and then added your spouse's name to the deed upon getting married—and your spouse helped with mortgage payments, built additions or made other contributions—it will no longer be regarded as your own separate property and will also be subject to division.

✓ Don't think no-fault means no-problem. While no-fault removes the acrimony of finding a "guilty" party, there will still be plenty of hassles about property division, alimony or child support. So keep your guard up.

✓ Maintain your own credit history. Keeping a credit card or two, a bank account and stocks and bonds under your own name means you will not be liable—or you will be less liable—for your spouse's debts in a divorce. Apply for a credit card under your own name if you do not have one.

✓ Don't allow your spouse, or your spouse's attorney, to intimidate you. Ignore threats like "if you don't accept this, you'll get nothing." Fight, with your attorney's help, for what you believe you deserve, and don't be pressured into a quicker—and unfair—settlement.

✓ Don't start your own business—or take a share in a business—when you are in the midst of a divorce. Otherwise, bingo!, you've just created another piece of marital property, subject to division in divorce.

✓ Contest a divorce action initiated by your spouse—even if you want a divorce—as a negotiating strategy, instead of filing a counterclaim. Thus, if your spouse is desperate for a quick divorce to marry a paramour, he or she may be willing to give in to some of your demands (*Cupids, Couples and Contracts*, by Lester Wallman and Sharon McDonnell).

DIVORCE SHOWERS?

After being part of a married couple, returning to single life is difficult for even the strongest of women. "A divorce shower is a interesting coping strategy," says Dr. Roxanne Cohen Silver, Associate Professor of Psychology and Social Behavior, University of California at Irvine.

But Cohen points out that a divorce shower is not a celebration. Instead, it's a time for friends food and, of course, gift-giving—which is a very practical idea considering the division of community property that typically comes with divorce (*Woman's Day*).

DO I DARE DATE?

Do not put your social life on the back burner! Parents who are newly single have a lot of questions and concerns about how to have an adult social life without neglecting their children. According to Dr. Anna Beth

Benningfield, President of the Association of Marriage and Family Therapists, making time for a social life is the hardest thing!

It is essential for an adult to maintain an adult social life that does not include the children (whether you're married or single). Children are not supposed to be included in all of their parents' activities. Parents sometimes forget this fact especially if they are very involved at work and they start to feel guilty about not spending enough time with the kids.

MEET THE KIDS?

If and when you do meet someone, when is the right time to introduce him or her to your kids?

According to Dr. Benningfield, parents must remember that children, particularly young children, become easily attached to people. It can be confusing for your child if you are introducing your child to different acquaintances and then they never see him or her again. Dr. Benningfield advises that if you are considering introducing your child to someone that you are going to be seeing on a regular basis, then it is fine to bring him or her to dinner or a family barbecue.

SPENDING THE NIGHT

Spending the night away from home is different than spending the night at home with someone. If your current person is someone whose permanency in your life has not yet been determined, it may not be a good idea to tell your children the truth. I'm not advocating an out-and-out lie, but you have to remember that children are not entitled to all the details. Certainly their baby-sitter or care-taker should know how to reach you, but not necessarily the children themselves. As an adult, you have to use some discretion about how much information you give to your children. We have to remember that we are role models and what's going on in the parents' lives is likely to become a kind of blueprint for what goes on in a teen's life. You don't want your children to think that it's okay to have many sexual partners.

HOW'S THE DATING GAME GOING?

After my discussion with Anna Beth, we took a few calls on the radio show on the subject of singles and dating:

> Mary Jean, Englewood, Fl.: "One day, while waiting for a date to arrive, I had to run out unexpectedly to the store. I left my 11-year-old son behind to greet my date and offer him a seat. Upon arrival, he agreed to a game of 'cops and robbers' with my son. When I came back, the guy was tied to the chair. Needless to say, I never saw him again."

> Denise, Edison, NJ: "I am a single parent. I go to school full time and I work full time. Before accepting a date, I have to check my school schedule to make sure I don't have homework that particular weekend. And when I do date,

my kids, aged 20 and 17, start acting like drill sergeants. They check how I look, what I'm wearing, how I'm going to sit, who I'm going to talk to. And I can't bring anybody home!"

Your List

It's time to be business-like about this. Put down the names and phone numbers of all good prospective dates. Then list the best places to meet single people—suggestions from friends and magazine articles are good sources for these. Also list the most interesting ways to meet single people. Why write them down? Because just when you need a good idea the most, your brain will draw a blank—I guarantee it!

_____

_____

_____

_____

_____

_____

_____

_____

_____

_____

_____

3

Mother/ Parent

"When my kids become wild and unruly, I use a nice, safe playpen. When they're finished, I climb out."

—ERMA BOMBECK

an you believe you are a parent? The most amazing discovery about your parents becomes totally clear when you become one—they really DIDN'T KNOW what the hell they were doing either, though as a kid you never doubted them for a moment. The tough thing about being a parent is that you were just a kid yourself a minute ago, you just look older and have to act accordingly (whatever that is). I call it punting—trust me, no other parent really knows what's going on either. Being a good parent means making decisions on a daily basis that enable your children to grow up happy, healthy, safe and knowledgeable.

DEBnotes

✓Our decisions should never jeopardize our children's lives.

✓ We'll do anything to keep our kids from pain.

✓ We've got to try our hardest to instill good values.

✓ We need to be approachable.

✓ We need to be good to ourselves in order to be able to be good for them.

HARRIED MOM?

✓ Find a place that soothes, calms and restores you—a window seat, an attic room, and use it when you need some solitude.

✓ At the end of the day, remind yourself of one thing you did in the last 24 hours that made you feel proud.

✓ Pursue a new interest—gardening, a book club—something that has nothing to do with being a wife or mother.

✓ During harried times of your day, don't accept telephone interruptions or visits from friends or relatives.

✓ Maintain your physical self with weekly home facials, bubble baths and exercise.

✓ Let go of three shoulds that don't really need to be done (*McCall's*).

CONFLICTING EMOTIONS

The Benedict Arnold Syndrome is a phrase I use to describe the love-hate feelings you can have toward your kids in the same half hour. Of course, there's much more love but, I'll tell you, they can make you turn on them in a split second. If this happens, don't worry, it's perfectly natural. I've discussed this topic with many other mothers and they all admit it's a common occurrence. Notwithstanding how normal it is, it can still bring you right to the edge, can't it? That's when you really must exercise self-control, not controlling your responses to them—ALLOWING them to bring out the worst in you—is the difference between a good mom and a rotten one.

DISCIPLINE

According to a *USA Today* poll, parents who discipline thier children use the following techniques:

✓ Time-out 65%
✓ Spanking 20%
✓ Both 8%
✓ Other 7%

DEB*tips:*

✓ There is no magic formula for disciplining your child. But here are some steps to help you guide your children with love and firmness, based on Stephanie Marston's book, *Work and Family Life*.

✓ Take time to think before acting or reacting. When we respond under pressure, we often say things we later regret. With time to think, we can be less reactive and more effective in how we discipline our kids.

✓ Encourage cooperation. Motivating children is another key to effective discipline. When the relationship with our kids becomes a series of power struggles, we're bound to lose. Given half-a-chance, children want to please us and be positive, contributing family members. At the same time, they're exploring their own individuality. If we continually enforce our point-of-view, they will instinctively resist—and we end up in an ongoing battle of wills. If the child always wins, we'll have an out-of-control child. If we always win, our child's individuality will be suppressed or defeated.

✓ All children's actions are aimed at getting their needs met. This may be hard to remember in the heat of the moment, but it's still true whether or not a child's behavior is acceptable. When your child misbehaves, ask yourself how can you help your child get his or her needs met in a more positive way.

✓ A misbehaving child is a discouraged child, and the way to help is to be as encouraging as you can. Encouragement is to children what water is to a plant—they need it to grow and blossom. You can always find something to praise about your children's strengths and talents, such as, "You're putting in a lot of time studying for your English test," or "I appreciate the way you included your sister in the game."

HOLD POSITIVE EXPECTATIONS

Do you describe your child as lazy? Cooperative? Immature? Competent? Kids are sensitive about our attitudes toward them. If you perceive children as responsible and cooperative, you will give them more opportunities to demonstrate their competence. And the more trust and confidence you place in them, the more they learn they are worthy of trust and the more trustworthy they become. We need to consciously train ourselves to hold positive, yet realistic expectations for our children. We need to let kids know we believe they're capable and that we will support them as they in develop and grow.

IGNORING WHAT'S UNIMPORTANT

Not every problem requires an intervention. A lot of situations can be ignored and in many cases children will stop their inappropriate behavior as soon as you stop paying attention to it. Find your own balance between ignoring and intervening. We can probably ignore most minor misbehaviors: sibling arguments, whining, getting dirty, spilling milk, goofiness, or refusing to eat. Frequently kids persevere with behavior to get a reaction. That's why it's often better to ignore what you can tolerate and save your energy for important issues.

POPULARITY WITH OTHER KIDS

Remember, that the way you discipline your child will not only affect your relationship, but it also will determine the way your child reacts to his or her peers.

Psychologist Dr. Craig Hart recently led a research team at Louisiana State University in a study of 106 three-to five-year olds. These children were observed playing with their peers in their preschool's playground. The children's parents were then interviewed about their discipline techniques.

The investigators found that the most popular children had mothers who set clear limits, explained consequences and encouraged their preschoolers to develop good judgment. For example, if a child was arguing with a playmate about who goes down the slide first, these mothers would be likely to say, "What could you do so that each of you can have a turn going first?"

This type of intervention is in sharp contrast to those mothers who, in the same situation, were apt to exert control by yelling "Stop fighting or we'll go home right now!" Not surprisingly, the least popular children were those who followed Mom's lead by yelling, threatening and hitting.

The results of this study indicate that children tend to treat peers the same way they are treated at home and this can affect their ability to make and sustain friendships (*Working Mother* magazine).

ARE YOU APPROACHABLE?

According to Faber and Mazlish's book, *How to Talk So Kids will Listen and Listen So Kids Will Talk*, if your responses match any of those listed below, your child may not find you approachable:

✓ Commanding responses: "Clean up your room right now."
✓ Threatening responses: "If you don't stop yelling, I'm going to...."
✓ Criticizing: "That doesn't look like an "S" to me."
✓ Name-calling: "Jane's just lazy."
✓ Blaming: "It's your fault that we're late."
✓ Interrogating: "Who were you with? Why didn't you call? How did you get dirty?"
✓ Sarcasm: "You call this clean?"
✓ Comparing: "Hank is the smart one."

SINGLE PARENT

Being a single parent, which is my official status, definitely changes the deal! Talk about pressure ... keeping the relationship with the "ex" civil, figuring out the weekend arrangements and whatnot, managing a new relationship—however wonderful it may be—there are a lot of burdens when you are a single parent.

According to *Working Woman* magazine, eight million homes in this country are headed by single mothers. There's a single mom stereotype, too—unique, unpleasant and unfortunate. Yet single-parent families are as diverse and as similar as any other kind of family. They're large and small, demonstrative and reserved, neat and sloppy, even rich and sometimes broke.

The 1990 U.S. Census figures show that nearly 400,000 families are headed by single mothers who earn $50,000 or more; and another 1.5 million make $30,000 or more. However, the median income for women heads of households was $13,000.

According to a *USA Today* survey, 50 percent of single women with children feel burned out from their jobs, while 31 percent of working married women do.

SINGLE PARENTING ON A SHOESTRING BUDGET

✓ When visiting the doctor, stock up on samples. Don't wait for your child to get a runny nose, fever or rash and then rush to the pharmacy to buy expensive over-the-counter preparations. Ask your doctor to fill up a bag of pain relievers, ointments, decongestants and antihistamines.

✓ Lunches. Pack lunches for your kids instead of sending them off with money—you'll save over $200 a year.

✓ Live a simple life. Think about how much you and your family require, and sift out frills and excess. If you're eligible for welfare, child support or any other type of financial assistance, by all means get it! If, however, you are ineligible for public assistance yet can still only barely make ends meet, take inventory and see what you and your family absolutely need. A good resource publication for single mothers is *Single Mother*, produced by the National organization of Single Mothers, 704-888-KIDS.

✓ Think you can't afford a vacation? Consider the way many European families travel—they stay at youth hostels instead of expensive hotels. Travel this way can provide some interesting adventures on an "interesting" budget. For more information, call the American Youth Hostels headquarters at 202-783-6161.

✓ Single-parent dinner swap. One night a week, one single parent invites another single parent over for dinner. After dinner, the "guest" parent leaves to shop, study or just take some personal time—while leaving their kid(s) to play with your kid(s). The guest Mom gets one night where she doesn't have to deal with kids, meals, dishes or wiping the counter forty times! (*Working Mother* magazine.)

PREGNANCY

Some of the questions I asked myself when I was pregnant were: Will I ever have sex again? A waist? What comes first? I was 212, which was "two twelve"—as in two hundred and twelve pounds! After I gave birth to my beautiful 7-pound, 12-ounce girl, I said, "Check again—there must be something else in there." I was as big as an Italian female sumo wrestler. It was a shame I couldn't just keep the boobs. The highlight of my postpartum experience came when I was down somewhere around 185 pounds, and a group of foreign men riding in a pickup truck beeped and made a lewd comment. Secretly, I was thrilled because it meant that I must have at least resembled a woman.

While in labor, I chose the birthing chair, which turned out to be like a bad amusement park ride. My first comments after giving birth—"She's very nice, I'll meet her later. Boy, I need a scotch and a cigarette."

DEB*servation:* If you're a woman backing up to a fast food restaurant at 70 miles per hour after having just left the last one minutes before, chances are you're pregnant. Just three words on this topic—it's no joke!

DEB*tip:*

Follow your food cravings even if they lead to a temporary diet of potato chips and lemonade. Potato chips and other salty foods stimulate thirst, which helps women get the fluids they need. Lemon seems to quiet queasiness. Watch out for odors, they can sometimes trigger morning sickness. Some of the worst offenders are cigarette smoke, perfume and coffee that's been on the burner too long. To help avoid these odors carry something aromatic like lemon wedges, vanilla extract, an herbal tea bag or pine needles in a scarf or hankie (*Working Mother* magazine).

NAUSEA AD NAUSEUM

According to an article in *Baby Talk* magazine, a good thing for nausea is accupressure wristbands. Based on the Chinese theory that stimulating specific parts of the body can bring health benefits, these have a small bump that exerts pressure at a point on the wrist that is believed to quell nausea. Available in drug and mass merchandise stores around the country, or write to the Traveler's Checklist, 335 Cornwall Bridge Road, Sharon, Conn.

The Mask: Some women develop melasma during pregnancy, a condition in which facial skin pigment darkens, which can become aggravated by sun exposure. This is commonly referred to as the mask of pregnancy because darkening occurs only on the upper areas of the face. To minimize the severity of melasma, use sunscreens faithfully and limit your time in the sun.

PREGNANCY TIPS

✓ Eat before you begin to feel nauseous.
✓ The less you eat, the less nourishment your baby receives.
✓ Not gaining weight will not make preg nancy easier.
✓ Toxemia, a potentially serious condition of pregnancy, can be caused by maternal mal nutrition.

✓ Your baby will turn out exactly as you cre
ate it during your pregnancy.

✓ Moderate water retention is normal and a
good sign of being proper nourishment.

✓ You are at risk for malnutrition if you
smoke, drink, do drugs or are a vegetarian.

✓ Ideal weight gain is 20 to 27 pounds.

✓ Huge doses of Vitamin A can cause birth
defects.

✓ Huge doses of vitamin C also can cause
problems.

✓ Cravings may mean you are deficient in
some nutrients.

✓ Refined sugar is not good for your baby
(Tips from The Better Infomation Group).

─────

DEBtip:
Drink raspberry leaf tea. Don't ask me why,
just trust me, this stuff has something that
helps during pregnancy.

Actually, I first heard about the tea at my Lamaze class.
It seems to have been around all through the ages and is
recommended to women to help ensure a problem-free
pregnancy and smooth delivery. What's there to lose? It's
herbal tea, caffeine-free and it tastes delicious. Of course
there's a footnote here, you drink a cup a day until the
actual labor begins, at which point you steep something
like a small pillowcase full of this loose tea in a pint of
water. The idea is for it to be super strong, and you're

supposed to drink the whole pint straight down to make labor go faster. I actually did this in the emergency room parking lot at 5 a.m.

Well, I've only had one kid and the labor lasted about five hours—not bad! I was convinced that without the tea, I'd have been one of those hallway stalkers, you know, the ones hooked up to the I.V.'s walking up and down the halls praying for the end to come!

Your List of Doctors and Specialists

NAME	ADDRESS	PHONE

Dates of Tests

TEST	DATE	TIME	PLACE

Monthly Weight Gain (Now here's a fun chart!)

1st	2nd	3rd	4th	5th	6th	7th	8th	9th

BABIES

Everyone who has had a baby has done something really stupid at least once that had the potential to ruin the child for life. I'll never forget the day my three-month-old daughter rolled off the bed onto the floor while I was putting on pair of pantyhose. I swear I hadn't taken my eyes off her for more than a second before I heard a thump. At first I couldn't imagine what happened, but then the screams made it crystal clear. For the rest of the day until my husband came home, I was sure I'd caused her to be brain damaged for life.

She cried and I cried and we managed to survive—until the next day, when it happened again. This time I almost had myself taken away sure that I was a Mother misfit. It was the same head smash, slightly different circumstances. Anyway all's well—the only problem with her head now is that it's her own, containing her very own brain which makes its very own decisions. They're not always in sync with mine—some would call this being thick headed, so would I.

DEB*fact:*
Most newborns cry for a total of 60 to 90
minutes a day! Good Luck!

DEB*fact:*

What does a hungry cry sound like? It's usually quite rhythmic, repeating a cry—pause—cry—pause pattern.

FOOD

Breast milk is the best nutrition for your newborn. When babies are four-to-six months old, infant rice or barley cereals are good to start them on, adding a little fruit or vegetables to the diet as well. Babies don't need a wide variety of foods, stay with what they prefer. While you can overfeed a baby, they almost never overeat on their own. Let the baby decide when to stop. Remember the roots of obesity begin in childhood.

Because of their high allergic potential, don't feed your baby eggs, citrus fruits (including tomatoes), corn, or peanuts during the first year (*Baby Talk* magazine).

IMPORTANT LISTS

Keep track of things such as:

✓ Chart your baby's weight and height
✓ Sizes of clothes and shoes
✓ Dates they did something cute
✓ Friends' babies names and ages
✓ People you still have to thank for gifts

_____

_____

_____

_____

TEARS

Babies have their own unique crying patterns to convey hunger, discomfort and other distress messages. Some common cues can help you decipher your infant's needs. In general, loud inconsolable crying usually signals pain or an illness. If you're unable to comfort your baby, check for other symptoms such as fever, and consult a doctor.

By contrast, low intensity crying is most likely due to less serious causes, such as boredom or a wet diaper, and will quickly stop once a parent intervenes. Tears signaling hunger are often accompanied by finger sucking and mouth movements. And infants who are tired may cry for five or 10 minutes before falling asleep.

If an otherwise healthy baby under three months of age cries excessively without explanation, he or she may have colic. Though infants eventually outgrow this condition, you should consult your pediatrician (*McCall's*).

DR. SPOCK'S TIPS FOR COLIC RELIEF

Twenty percent of babies experience the pain and crying caused by colic. The condition usually emerges gradually about two weeks after birth. The crying turns into sharp, non-stop screams and during this period the abdomen becomes swollen and hard, and the baby passes gas frequently. Colic attacks come on almost every night without fail, beginning in the early evening and lasting about three-to-four hours.

The exact cause of colic is unknown, but one explanation, says Dr. Benjamin Spock, is that it's at least partly a normal, developmental stage that babies go through, given the consistent time frame in which it occurs. Some think it is caused by the immaturity of the digestive system. But, even in extreme cases a solution that might not work one day might provide relief the next. Dr. Spock's advice for stopping the tears include: Switching the baby off cow's milk formula. Nursing mothers can also pass along the protein in cow's milk if they consume it and other dairy products.

In addition to diet, motion can sometimes help: rocking, walking, driving in the car, carrying the baby in a sling. A hot water bottle filled with warm water could be soothing on the baby's tummy. Although colic is distressing for everyone, Dr. Spock reassures us that it usually lasts only about 90 days and leaves the baby with no lasting signs of unhappiness or stress (*Parenting* magazine).

THE NEW MOTHER MARKET STUDY

A national survey of new mothers conducted by *Baby Talk* magazine reported that most are working and two-thirds of working moms planned to return to work after the baby was born. More than half of the working mothers said they would gladly work and let their husbands stay a home if his salary were smaller. The survey also showed that 38% had paid baby-sitters (either in the sitter's home or with relatives); 31% report their husband or partner as caregiver; 17% are using child-care centers; 12% report a paid baby-sitter in their own home; and only 1% have live-in caregivers.

DEB*tips:*

✓ Every mother will agree that there are some days when you feel overwhelmed by the stress and responsibility of taking care of a baby. Try to take yourself and the baby out of the house for a walk, anywhere. You're allowed to take a break. Enlist a friend, relative, or sitter for a little private time. Don't be afraid to ask for help. You'll be a better mom if you take care of yourself.

✓ Make use of videos. Every mother needs a reprieve. Actually your usually just trying to find a minute to take a shower. So, watch for which ones pull a smile and load up—BARNEY, or Lambchop, or whatever it takes to buy some time. Other mothers will happily make video suggestions .

NAME THAT BABY

"Unisex monikers such as Taylor, Jordan and Alex are hot," says Susan Eyres, owner of a personal naming service. Eyres actually helps parents find the perfect name for their baby and reports that among her clients place names such as Dallas and Dakota are popular. Last names used as first names, such as Connor and Holden also are in. Other best-sellers for boys: Cody, Austin, Dylan, Colin, Hunter, Spencer and Garrett. Popular names for girls: Haylie, Caylin, Taryn, Kelsey, Carissa and McCaela. Traditionalists will be happy to hear there's still a demand for old favorites like Emily, Rebecca, Sarah, Jacob, Matthew and Daniel. Still stumped when it comes to finding just the right name? Eyres charges $45 for a list of 50 custom-picked names. Write to Sue's Names, 675 Mira Mesa Boulevard, Suite 123-262 San Diego, CA 92121 (*Working Mother* magazine).

UPDATE ON SIDS

According to Australian researchers at the University of Tasmania, overheated rooms, soft mattresses and tight coverings all increase the risk of sudden infant death syndrome (SIDS) for babies who sleep on their stomachs.

SIDS occurs most frequently in two-to-four months old infants. The American Academy of Pediatrics now advises that babies this age be placed on their side or back to sleep. If a baby must sleep on its stomach, he or she should be placed on a firm mattress, unswaddled and in a moderately cool room.

POTTY TRAINING

I'm embarrassed to admit I don't even remember my daughter's potty training experience. I do remember buying the cute little white potty, putting it in next the bathroom and dusting it every once in awhile. If I remember correctly, I think I even tried to make it a planter at one point—why waste it?

Last November, Kimberly-Clark Corporation, the company that makes the training pants, sponsored a contest on my radio show (The Working Mom on The Run) asking for favorite potty training tales. Well, the response was fantastic and some of the stories were hysterical.

Charlene from Fairfax Station, Virginia, wrote in to tell about what a difficult time she had with her son, Matt.

"Three year-old Matt, is the youngest of three brothers, and he delights in his position as the 'baby.' Although he displays obvious readiness for potty training in terms of intellect, physical maturity, verbal and motor skills, he stubbornly refuses to use the potty consistently and remains content to soil himself. At the same time, he talks excitedly about other 'big boy' milestones and likes to enumerate the many things that he, as a 'big boy' three years-old can do. Hoping to capitalize on this 'big boy' theme, his determined mother tried reminding Matt that 'big boys' also use the potty. 'You don't use the potty, Matt, so what does that make you?'" she asked pointedly. "Happy," Matt retorted.

Ironically, Matt's aunt, is none other than "Dr. Mom," Marianne Neifert of *McCall's* magazine who offers these tips for effectively potty training your child:

1. Potty training will be easier if parents are aware that training starts well before buying and using the potty. When parents promptly change their child's diaper as a baby, they indicate to the child that it feels good to be clean and dry. That message will stay with them until it comes time for potty training.

When parents don't change a diaper right away, the child won't know any differently at potty training time—they won't be able to recognize that they've made a "mess" and should have used the potty.

2. Look for signs of readiness in your child. The child has to be ready before he or she can be potty trained. A lot of parents forget this, and sometimes they hurry the process because of the pressure of child care centers to only enroll potty-trained children.

How can you tell if your child is ready? Children have to have their motor skills developed in order for them to even get to a potty. If a child does not have these abilities, parents should be patient and postpone their potty training efforts. In addition, a child should be able to verbalize when they have to use the potty. If a child can't do that, it is unrealistic to think that the child is ready for toilet training.

3. Potty training is a power struggle

between the child and parent. Instead of asking the child if they need to go potty, because your child may say "no" just to be belligerent, parents should watch for signs, particularly facial expressions, and immediately grab the child, saying "looks like you need to go potty." This spares both parent and child the frustration of sitting and waiting on the potty.

4. Many times potty training can become a power struggle when there is a younger child in the house. Kids see how a baby gets all of the attention while they're supposed to be the "big boy or girl." Who wants to do a big boy or girl thing if it means that they will get even less attention than their little brother or sister? Parents should be very encouraging and use lavish amounts of praise to influence their child to use the potty.

5. Parents should be understanding. Dr. Neifert says child abuse occurs most often over potty training accidents. Too many parents ignore it when their child does well and punish the child when there's an accident. Parents should expect accidents.

When kids have to go, believe them. But sometimes, when in a supermarket, mall or airport, you are not accessible to the rest room. Don't blame the child.

KIDS CLOTHES

DEB*servation:* I still have outfits for my daughter with the tags on! She blew past the size without ever wearing the stuff.

DEB*tip:*

Hanna Andersson, the children's mail-order-clothing company, features clothes for newborns to teens plus a few items for Mom. If you return used Hanna Andersson clothing in good condition, you get a credit of 20% of the purchase price, and they deliver the used clothing to a charity. It's a great idea for kids who outgrow clothes like lightening. Call 800-222-0544.

I've mentioned consignment and thrift shops in this book and on the show. Recently I read in *Woman's Day* about consignment events. These are giant two- to-seven-day sales of used kids' clothing (and toys, baby equipment and maternity clothes), which take place in the spring or fall. Church groups or Moms who want to make extra cash usually run the sales, signing up sellers and setting up the place and time. Moms who come to sell earn about two-thirds of the price of their items (consignment shops usually keep one half), and may also enjoy the privilege of early bird shopping at preview sales. Moms who come just to shop discover great bargains and a vast selection of kid's clothes. The trick is finding these sales, which attract participants largely by word-of-mouth. Browse newspaper ads and church and community center bulletin boards or just ask around.

Your List (Better write in pencil!)

	Kid #1	Kid #2	Kid #3	Kid #4
Coat				
Gloves				
Shirt/blouse				
Pants				
Dress				
Shoes/Socks				
Underwear				

OFF TO SCHOOL

I will continue to hit new lows as to how I allow myself to walk out of the house in the morning to take my daughter to school. Fortunately the other mothers are just as ugly. In fact it's THE UGLY BRIGADE—but for those few maniacal types who must get up at four to do the whole dolled up thing and then most likely go home and see nobody else the rest of the day.

"You can't take their test or hold their hands, but you can make a difference in how your children feel about and perform in school."

—DIANNE HALES

Parents are key to their kids' success in school. "Make school interesting by being interesting yourself," suggests Marguerite Kelly, author of a syndicated column called "The Family Almanac." Kelly urges that you talk about ideas at dinner. Chat about stories in the newspapers. Discuss movies you've seen or books you've read. Express your opinions and ask your children for theirs.

Provide a quiet, comfortable study area. Each child needs a flat writing surface, a firm chair and basic materials, such as pencils, pens and paper. With each grade, your kids will need more reference materials, such as a globe, dictionaries and an encyclopedia.

Treat homework seriously. Be realistic and compassionate, but also be firm. This advice comes from Nancy Honig, founder and president of the Quality Education Project in California. Some children are easily frustrated and need to be told, "Calm down, try again, you can do it." Others need to be reminded that the sooner they complete their work, the better they'll feel about themselves and school and the more hours they'll have for "fun time."

Monitor homework daily, but don't do the work yourself. Discuss each child's assignments and offer suggestions for organizing time and breaking down tasks into steps.

DEB*news:*

Thirty years of research shows that 90 percent
of a child's achievement in school is determined by the amount of TV he or she watches,
school attendance and how much reading is

done at home. Studies have also shown that
parental involvement is more important to
academic success than a family's income level.

———

Have each child read to you for 15 minutes every day.
"The point is not to teach a child to read," Honig
explains, "but to listen attentively." Set a regular reading
time, such as before bed every night. "No matter how
poor a reader a child may be, there will be obvious
improvement in a few weeks," says Honig. "Even more
worthwhile will be your child's increased self-esteem."

Praise your kids. Always look for positives: finishing
homework without reminders from you or knowing how
to spell all the words on the spelling list. Also let your
children know you love them just for being themselves.
"Feeling good can make a child soar—in school and at
home," says Honig.

Attend parent-teacher conferences, open houses, etc.
You'll find out a lot about the school, be able to monitor
your kids' progress better and show them that their education is important to you.

PARENT-TEACHER CONFERENCES

Parents magazine encourages parents to "make the
most of your parent-teacher conference," describing the
face-to-face meetings as a precious opportunity to
improve your child's education.

Here's some tips on how to establish a partnership with your child's teacher:

✓ Think about what you want to ask and what you want the teacher to know.

The day before the conference, ask your child which are his or her favorite subjects, which he or she likes least, and why. Make two lists. One with questions that you want to ask the teacher, the other with information that you want to give the teacher about your child. Sample questions include: What is the daily routine in your classroom? Can you show me some samples of my child's work? How do you track my child's progress? Does my child participate in class discussions and activities? Does he or she work well independently? How can I enhance learning at home? What is the best way for me to keep in touch with you throughout the school year?

On the other list, write down your child's particular interests or needs. For example, let the teacher know if your child loves the after-school art lessons or is afraid to go out on the playground. Let him or her also know about family matters that might affect your child's behavior, such as a new baby, an illness in the family or a divorce or separation.

✓ Start the conference off on a positive note.

The best way to start a conference is with a comment of appreciation. The teacher will surely brighten if you make a comment such as, "Ben really enjoys your class." Even, "I like your bulletin board" helps set a positive tone.

By the first conference, the teacher can tell you how your child is progressing academically and socially. The teacher should be able to tell you whether your child is working at, above, or below grade level. It is also important to clarify your teacher's grading system and what the grades mean.

✓ **Handle disagreements with the teacher without being confrontational.**

If you disagree with the teacher's assessment of your child or think one of your child's grades is unfair, first ask for specific examples of the work or behavior. Sometimes your differences with the teacher won't be so easily resolved. What if the teacher won't take your concern seriously or becomes defensive?

One important rule, according to Claude Goldenberg, Ph.D. associate professor at the School of Education at California State University, Long Beach, is to make sure that you state your criticism in non-threatening language. For example, start with "I've noticed that," or "I'm concerned about." Then explain the problem in a way that presents you as an ally working toward the same goal. If, after a week or so, you feel that issues brought up in the conference haven't been resolved, schedule another conference in two or three weeks.

DEB*alert:*

DO NOT wait until parent-teacher conferences to become involved with your kid's school.

Last June, I had the pleasure of chatting with talk show host Montel Williams on "The Working Mom on the Run." Although his two children are not school age, Montel has had a lot of experience with families during his career as a talk show host and motivational speaker. We both feel very strongly about parents taking the time—and employers allowing their employees to take the time—to visit their children's school(s).

It's incredible that so few parents actually go to their child's school at all or know what is going on in the course of a day. They just send their kids off and go on about their own matters. I thought about this the other day ... I send my kid off each day to be with strangers, who we assume are fine because the teachers are accredited. Who knows what goes on from the time I leave her in the morning until the afternoon? Unless you go by there and participate, you don't know the pattern of the child's day and you can't really even talk intelligently with your child about what is going on.

Finally, some good news for working parents—change

is in the works! The Family-School Partnership Act assembly bill is a "family friendly" policy that went into effect on January 1, 1995, in California. The law was authored by Delaine Eastin, State Superintendent of Public Instruction and guarantees parents time off work to participate in their children's school activities.

It covers employers who have 25 or more employees at the same location. Parents, guardians, or grandparents who have custody of children can take up to 40 hours off each school year, but no more than eight hours in any month, as long they give their employer reasonable notice. Previous law had applied only to privately owned firms and had allowed only four hours during the entire school year.

KIDS AND SPORTS

One of the greatest things a parent can experience in life is the knowledge that their kid is great at sports! A champion, physically superior, a contender, a team player—MY KID!

This could get ugly, however, if the coach or other adult in charge of this part of your kid's existence doesn't see it quite the same way.

HOW TO MANAGE A DIFFICULT COACH

If a coach gets obsessed with winning and losing, and loses his perspective on the fact that he's coaching children as opposed to, say, the New York Yankees, you should call the coach or meet him off the field to discuss the situation. In a non-argumentative way, discuss your concern for his behavior. Don't make a scene at the game by confronting the coach because this will alienate the coach and embarrasses your child.

Remember to tell your child that the most important thing to you is that he or she has fun playing and that both winning and losing are part of any game. You shouldn't confront your child or yell when his or her team loses.

If a coach allows only the best players to play and benches the others, you should remind the coach that every child should be allowed to play. You shouldn't be passive. All kids would rather play than warm a bench.

If a coach yells obscenities during the game, you should say to the coach, "We don't use that kind of language in my household, and I don't appreciate your using it around my child" (*Child* magazine).

List of the "other kids," their parents, and the names and phone numbers of coaches for each sport:

_____

_____

_____

_____

_____

_____

_____

_____

_____

TIPS FOR YOUNG ATHLETES' PARENTS

1. Winning is great but striving to win is more important.
2. Attitude of athletes dictates outcome of experience.
3. Kid confidence becomes the foundation for adult character.
4. Equipment and sportswear maintenance prevents injury.
5. Manners count on and off the field/court.
6. Adult egos should be checked at the door.
7. Note that every successful adult had their start as a kid (David Blagys of Wakeman Boys and Girls Club).

GIRLS AND SPORTS

✓ 97% of coaches of young women's sports surveyed said that girls involved in sports are less likely to smoke than those who aren't, and 90% said the female athletes are less likely to have unplanned pregnancies.

✓ 79% of those same coaches said that female athletes don't feel they receive as much financial aid from sponsors as their male counterparts do. And 67% said that females don't feel they receive equal support in the form of money and facilities from school administrations (the Women's Sports Foundation Survey).

LET THE MUSIC PLAY

You can add to your child's success in the classroom and on the playing field by providing him or her with music lessons.

DEB*servation:* You don't have to listen—get ear plugs, cover them with your hair and keep smiling as long as their little hands are moving.

Working Mother magazine reports that music lessons can be worthwhile even if your child shows no innate talent. According to a recent study conducted by a research team at the University of California at Irvine, children who take music lessons become more proficient at non-verbal reasoning tasks.

The researchers studied three-year-old children who were given singing or music lessons for six months as part of their pre-school curriculum. They found these children were significantly more adept at intelligence test puzzle tasks than other three-year-olds.

The researchers suggest that music lessons help train kids to use the part of the brain responsible for non-verbal reasoning skills.

TEENS (ACNE AND AGIDA!)

DEB*servation:* Remember, our kids will probably try to pull all the things on us that we tried to pull on our parents. Think back—and be prepared.

Wisconsin psychologist Dr. Lawrence Steinberg says that parents suffer more than their kids through their kids' adolescence. Dr. Steinberg argues in his book, *Crossing Paths,* that teenagers "coast through life in a sort of pleasant fog" while parents feel tremendous upheaval. Parents experience deep feelings over a child's rapid growth, Dr. Steinberg writes, including the loss of physical control over their children and, most of all, watching an adolescent turn into a sexual being. This triggers in parents all kinds of conflicts about their own attractiveness, sexuality and marriage.

KEEP COMMUNICATION LINES OPEN

In order to make this extremely difficult time easier for parents and to foster a better relationship with their children, *Work and Family Life* suggests keeping communication open with your teenager.

Parents must understand that teens face many pressures that adults tend not to take seriously. Teenagers' bodies are undergoing dramatic changes. They worry about their personal safety, about divorce and death, and ask themselves, "who am I" and "what am I going to do with my life?"

Self-doubt, too, is constant. Teenagers feel pressure to conform and fear ridicule if they don't. This can be bewildering, frightening and even depressing. In light of all this, it helps to know that almost nine out of 10 adolescents get through their teen years with no serious trouble (nine out of 10 parents of teenagers are on Valium!— only kidding!)

GETTING ALONG WITH YOUR TEEN

✓ Listen. Really listen. Because working parents have so much to do and so little time, we often try to listen while we're cooking, cleaning or fixing the car. Put your chores aside so your teen knows you're really paying attention.

✓ Take the long view. Don't treat minor mishaps as major catastrophes. Pick the important issues. Don't make your home a battleground.

✓ Tolerate differences. View your teenager as an individual distinct from you. This doesn't mean you can't have an opinion if you disagree.

✓ Respect your teenager's privacy. However, if a particular behavior is worrying you, don't hesitate to speak up.

✓ Be generous with praise. Praise your child's efforts, not just accomplishments.

✓ Set reasonable limits. Teenagers need them. Your rules should be consistently applied and rooted in your deepest beliefs and values.

✓ Teach your teenager to make sensible decisions and choices by encouraging independence and letting him or her make mistakes. Don't step in unless you have to.

✓ Find an activity you enjoy doing together and pursue it. If your invitations are declined, keep asking (*Work and Family Life*).

DEB*memory*

As a teen, there was nothing worse than worrying what lurked behind the door when arriving
home past the dreaded "curfew." Would it be a
parent possessed? Or, by some great stroke of
luck, would they be sleeping?

Family Circle's publication of *Hints, Tips and Smart
Advice* offers the following tips on teens and curfew rules:

✓ Let an alarm clock monitor your son or daughter.
Set a clock for the agreed-upon time and place it inside
the front door. If your teen comes home before curfew,
she or he will turn off the alarm. If your teen is late, it
will go off and awaken you. Once there is no more room
for speculation about when your son or daughter gets
home, your teen will become amazingly prompt.

✓ Having more than one teenager and only one car
can cause problems too. Try a "reservation" system. Make
a calendar chart and post it on the refrigerator door. The
children write in their names on the date they want to
use the car. They also write what time they need the car,
where they are going and how long they'll be gone (you
can also have them put the number where they can be
reached for emergencies). The first person to reserve the
car for a particular day gets it. From looking at the chart
you can tell if one child is monopolizing the car, and
keep track of where everyone is. Best of all, there won't
be any question about identifying the culprit who left the
gas tank empty!

PROBLEMS WITH YOUR TEEN (BESIDES ACNE!)

According to *Work and Family Life* magazine, the following are signs to alert you to the need for outside help:

✓ Recent changes in sleeping or eating habits, thinking patterns, personality, friendships, study habits or grades.

✓ Suicidal talk of any kind. A suicidal teen may give away valued possessions, talk about death, make a will and say his family would be better without him. A sudden end to a long depression often precedes a suicide attempt.

✓ Most teenagers get depressed, but there's a big difference between mood swings and depression—so pay attention to the intensity and duration of depression.

✓ A recent change in friends who you feel may be involved with drugs or alcohol could indicate that your child also is involved or be a sign of other problems.

✓ Drug or alcohol use. You might notice: irrational or irresponsible behavior, lying, secretiveness, severe mood swings, a sudden increase in accidents.

✓ Listlessness, loneliness, withdrawal, difficulty making friends, poor self-image. Self-doubt is normal, but persistently low self-esteem is a problem.

✓ Problems at school including class cutting, absenteeism, a sudden drop in grades.

✓ Fears and anxieties that interfere with everyday activities.

DEBf*act:*

Is your teen obsessed with weight watching? About 90% of people with eating disorders are adolescent and young adult women.

According to the National Institute of Mental Health, eating disorders and treatment for them include:

✓ Anorexia nervosa: a preoccupation with dieting and thinness that leads to excess weight loss.

✓ Bulimia nervosa: a pattern of binge eating followed by purging and intense feelings of guilt and shame.

✓ Most people with eating disorders share certain personality traits: low self-esteem, feelings of helplessness and fear of becoming fat.

✓ Treatment for eating disorders usually includes an internist, a nutritionist or a psychologist who specializes in the disorders and a family psychotherapist.

For information, get in touch with the National Association of Anorexia Nervosa and Associated Disorders, P.O. Box 7, Highland Park, Il 60035, (708) 831-3438; or the American Anorexia/Bulimia Association, 425 East 61st Street, Sixth Floor, New York, NY 10021, 212-891-8686.

YIKES, TEEN SEX

Most teens today have sex before 20 (*USA Today*). "Sex and America's Teenager," a report from the Alan Guttmacher Institute, puts several decades of research on teen sex in one place and attempts to put it in context. The report says that teens do have sex earlier than ever though not as early as some adults suspect. One survey found that adults thought most teens had sex before 16 when, in fact, more than half are virgins at that age. The report does urge educators and parents to encourage the postponement of sex, but to deal with the fact that most teens eventually do have sex.

TALKING TO YOUR TEEN ABOUT SEX

✓ Don't be afraid to use personal examples.
✓ Give factual, nonevasive, nonjudgmental answers to any question your child asks.
✓ Give your child the opportunity to have private counseling (*McCall's*).

COLLEGE

Going away to college was probably one the greatest things that ever happened in my life. Of course, there was a huge—and I mean HUGE—problem when it came to convincing my father that I should actually move away from home to go. Of course he wanted the best for me and had worked hard to save money for me to go. He had hoped I'd go to a local college and come home at night. Thank goodness for his best friend, who had two kids that went away to college and who just happened to be scholars and athletes. Eventually my father gave in, and off I went to see Ithaca College—my first choice and final destination.

I flew up with my Mother and my Aunt Yolanda, who came for moral support. I'll never forget the excitement of seeing the gorgeous college campus, and I'll never forget the suffocating feeling in the elevator as we were touring the health facility. While trapped in the elevator, the moron campus guide—who obviously never had a Mother—announced with gleeful simple-mindedness the availability of birth control pills right in front of my Mother and Aunt Yolanda! I'd have killed but couldn't get away with it, so I kicked him instead—he deserved it!

WHERE TO GO

Here's *Money Magazine's* top 10 colleges based on cost, quality, faculty and library resources:

1. **New College, University of South Florida**
2. **Rice University, Texas**
3. **Trenton State College, New Jersey**
4. **State University of New York, Binghamton**
5. **Northeast Missouri State**
6. **Hanover College, Indiana**
7. **Rutgers, New Jersey**
8. **California Institute of Technology**
9. **Spellman College, Georgia**
10. **St. Mary's College, Maryland.**

GETTING YOUR KID IN COLLEGE OF CHOICE

The application gives the college its first impression of your child. A great book to help make the most of this pervasive first impression is, *Show! Don't Tell—How To Personalize College Applications*—a step-by-step guide through the application process, including 75 sample essays and resumes from 60 high school graduates who were accepted by colleges between 1985 and 1993. You'll also find writing by students who matriculated to the most competitive universities in the nation, as well as others who attended two-year community colleges. Fifteen percent of the profit from the book is being put aside for a scholarship fund, and your child could be eligible.

For more information, call 800-SHOW HOW, or write to International Editing, P.O. Box 257, Monroe, CT 06468.

GIRL KIDS IN COLLEGE

According to Secretary of Labor Robert Reich in an article written exclusively for *Working Mother* magazine, college educated women are the only group of workers whose income rose in the 1980s. In fact, recent reports show women college graduates earn more than half of all college graduates—an indication that they will continue to make economic gains in the coming years.

Officials of women's colleges have initiated aggressive marketing campaigns to trumpet their successes, claiming that their institutions produce a larger proportion of Ph.D's and leaders in government and business.

According to an article published in *The New York Times*, there is a distinct resurgence of applications to both women's colleges and girls high schools, which seems to be directly related to concerns over sexual harassment and beliefs by young women and their parents that girls are treated differently than boys in co-educational schools.

FINANCIAL AID

Financial aid eligibility is determined by the college financial aid office. The basic formula is: the total cost of college minus the anticipated family contribution. You should really make every effort to become buddy-buddy with the financial aid officers at the colleges you are considering.

ADDING THINGS UP

When considering the total cost of attendance, you should include the following:

✓ Tuition and Fees
✓ Books and Supplies
✓ Room and Board
✓ Personal expenses
✓ Transportation

When considering the your ability to contribute, include the following:

✓ Your income
✓ Your assets, i.e., percentage of the value of a business, savings, stocks and bonds and mutual funds.
✓ Student's income and assets, if relevant.

In order to be considered for financial aid, apply as soon as possible. It is best to apply for aid the same time you apply for admission.

WORKING STUDENTS

According to a *Money Magazine* article, students at Berea College in Kentucky work 10 to 14 hours a week at campus jobs in exchange for tuition grants. At the College of The Ozarks in Point Lookout, Mo., students pay their way by working on campus 15 hours a week.

HOW TO GO TO COLLEGE AT HOME

If you are self-employed or homebound raising children, getting a college degree at home is easier than ever before, according to *Good Housekeeping* magazine. A growing number of colleges have programs that allow students to earn undergraduate and graduate degrees at their own pace at home via computer, television and correspondence courses—and you might even be eligible to get credits for what you already know.

School Via Computer

If you have a computer and modem, you are equipped to take a course from any on-line computer program. Here are some on-line degree programs you can attend from anywhere in the country:

✓ Via computer, the University of Phoenix offers a Bachelor of Science and Master of Science in Business Administration, as well as Bachelor of Arts and Master of Arts in Management. For information, call 800-742-4742.

✓ The On-Line Campus of The New York Institute of Technology offers three Bachelor of Science degrees in Business Administration, Interdisciplinary Studies, and Behavioral Sciences. For information, call 800-222-6948.

✓ Boise State University offers a Master of Science in Instructional and Performance Technology. For information, call 800-824-7017, extension 4457.

✓ Connected Education Inc., in White Plains, N.Y., in conjunction with the New School for Social Research in New York City, offers a Master of Arts in Media Studies. For information, call 914-428-8766.

School Via Television

Television courses are usually supplemented with text-books and other course material. Here are a few national programs with a wide variety of courses:

✓ Mind Extension University. Available through basic cable, satellite, or videotape. Affiliated with 26 universities and offers a wide range of undergraduate and graduate courses. For information, call 800-777-6463.

✓ Public Broadcasting System Adult Learning Service. Offers a variety of liberal arts courses in collaboration with 2,000 colleges. Classes are broadcast on public TV or cable channels, and are also available on videotape. Ask your local colleges if they participate, or call the education director at your local public TV station.

Correspondence School

Most correspondence courses are for personal enrich-ment, but some are for college credit and there are some degree programs. For a list of correspondence schools, write the Distance Education and Training Council, 1601 18th Street, NW, Washington, D.C., 20009.

Getting Credit For What You Know

Ask the college you are planning to attend whether it will grant credit for the knowledge and experience you have. There are two avenues available: Credits by examination—you can take proficiency exams that might allow you to skip introductory courses; and credits for life experience, which are awarded for knowledge you have acquired through professional training, volunteer work, homemaking, travel, etc. You must be able to demonstrate that the knowledge you have acquired is equal to that of a college course. Contact the school you plan to attend for more information (*Good Housekeeping*).

Last but certainly not least—keep in touch with me! I am currently putting together a scholarship fund for working Mothers who want to go back to school.

You can reach me by writing: Debbie Nigro, P.O. Box 4005, Grand Central Station, New York, NY, 10163.

HELPFUL READING FOR COLLEGE FINANCIAL HELP

The Student Guide to Education, the U.S. Dept of Education, Consumer Information Center, Pueblo, CO 81009.

The College Cost Book, College Board, 45 Columbus Avenue, New York, NY 10023-6992. Available at most bookstores.

Best Buys In College Education, Edward B. Fiske, Times Books. Available at most bookstores.

Money Magazine's "Best College Buys Annual Edition." Pick it up at you local newsstand.

Lovejoy's Guide To Financial Aid, Robert Leider, Monarch Press. Available at most bookstores.

How to Find Out About Financial Aid: A Guide to Over 700 Directories Listing Scholarships, Fellowships, Loans, Grants, Awards, Internships, Gail A. Schlater.

The College Money Handbook 1990. The Only Complete Guide to Expenses, Scholarships and Loans, Jobs and Special Aid Programs at Four-Year Colleges.

Foundation Grants to Individuals, 6th edition. Foundation Center, New York, NY.

Higher Education Opportunities for Minorities and Women, the U.S. Department of Education, Assistant Secretary for Post Secondary Education. Washington, D.C.

For information about these books, call The Partnership Group, Inc. 800-847-5437.

4

Grandparents— Aren't They Grand?

*"My grandmother started walking
five miles a day when she was 60.
She's 97 now, and we don't know where
the hell she is."*

—ELLEN DEGENERES

I t's hard to believe these are the very same people who raised you. Sure, the edge had to come off sooner or later, and then voila´—grandchildren. Greatest thing since French toast, and they spoil them, bribe them, provide love on call. It's like the T-shirt says: "If I knew grandchildren were so much fun, I'd have had them first."

THERE GOES THE INHERITANCE ...

The nation's mature market of consumers—those 50 years old and up—is now 65 million strong. And in a typical month, half the grandparents in that market buy a present for a grandchild. It's the perfect set-up for "Gifts for Grandkids," a first-of-its-kind free catalog targeted at affluent grandparents.

The items are priced from $15 to $400, and range from building blocks to science kits. The catalog also includes a section on things to do with grandkids. For a catalog or more information, call 800-333-1707.

MORE (AND MORE) TIME WITH THE GRANDKIDS

Results from an ongoing National Institute on Aging study on health, work, the economic situation and the family relationships of more than 13,000 Americans born between 1931 and 1941, show that grandparents are spending more time than ever with their grandchildren, both for child care and for fun!

The study also found that the average time spent in grandchild care was a whopping 659 hours a year, which amounts to 82 eight-hour days—that translates to nearly two hours a day, every day.

A different survey, by Roper Starch Worldwide, indicates grandparents are also having a lot of fun with the kids! A little over a third had taken grandchildren to regular restaurants the month before the poll, and a similar proportion had taken them to fast food restaurants.

One-third of the survey respondents reported that they go shopping with their grandchildren during the month, and more 20 percent had take them on a trip or to movies, sports events, museums and other places (*Wall Street Journal*).

THE GRANDPARENT AS PARENT ... AGAIN

As of 1990, more than 3.3 million children live with their grandparents who are their primary caregivers or legal guardians—a 41% increase since 1980 according to the Census Bureau.

Some do this to assist working parents, while others seek custody because the parents neglect their children, suffer from mental or emotional problems, abuse drugs or alcohol, or, in the case of teen pregnancy, are too young to assume child care responsibilities. The challenges for grandparents? Increasing household expense and future tuition could force them to dip into retirement savings or to return to work. If they are already working they may have to quit a job. And running after kids can tax the stamina of an older person who may already face significant health problems.

HELP IS AVAILABLE

Grandparents may be entitled to financial aid and/or medical care for the children in their custody. *Good Housekeeping* magazine suggests the following resources:

✓ AARP Grandparent Information Center, 601 E. St NW, Washington, D.C. 20049. 202-434-2296.

✓ Foundation for Grand Parenting, Box 326, Cohasset, MA 02025 (Send a self-addressed business size envelope with 64 cents in postage for a copy of the "Vital Connections" newsletter).

✓ National Coalition of Grandparents, 137 Larkin Street, Madison, WI 53705. 608-238-8751.

✓ Rocking, Box 96, Niles, MI 49120. 616-683-9038.

Your List

List grandparents' addresses, phone numbers, birthdays, anniversaries and special likes and dislikes so you remember. Also, the names and numbers of their closest friends and neighbors in the event you can't reach them or need to check on them (bet you don't even have these numbers—now's a good time to get them!).

_____

_____

_____

_____

_____

_____

_____

_____

_____

_____

_____

ELDER CARE

"By 2020, one in three workers will provide some kind of care for an aged parent or other relative."

—ANDREW SCHARLACH, PROFESSOR OF AGING, THE UNIVERSITY OF CALIFORNIA AT BERKELEY

Okay, who figured it would happen? You knew your parents were going to get older but you never really believed it. This whole thing is really out of your league, but if ever you had to step to the plate, it's now. Whether they don't want to burden you, or they are a complete pain and make your life miserable, you love them and are responsible for them. And, you could probably use some help.

As the oldest baby boomers approach their fifties, managers can expect to see elder care replace child care as the number-one dependent care issue for employees. An estimated 10%-15% of all workers are struggling to balance work and the often overwhelming responsibility of caring for aging or ill relatives (*USA Today*).

✓ The average American woman spends 17 years raising children and 18 years helping aging parents (U.S. House of Representatives Report 1988).

✓ Nearly seven million Americans provide unpaid personal care to elderly friends and family members (AARP and The Travelers).

✓ One-third of employees say they work less effectively than they could because of child and elder care (Families and Work Institute).

✓ Nearly two million women care for children and aging parents (D&B Reports).

✓ In a survey of 33 companies, 55% of the women and 50% of the men surveyed reported being interrupted at work as a result of their elder-care responsibilities (Regional Research Institute for Human Services).

✓ For information about child and elder care, call the National Council of Jewish Women at 800-622-NCJW.

AID FOR ELDERLY CARETAKERS

Thirty-five percent of the estimated 7 million caregivers to the elderly are over 65 themselves—and they need help, too. A new resource, *The Eldercare Locator*, can put them in touch with community agencies that provide adult day care, meal deliveries, legal services, transportation and more. For help or information, call U.S. Administration On Aging hotline Monday through Friday 9 a.m. to 11 p.m. at 800-677-1116.

THE MORE, THE BETTER

When looking at a nursing facility, look for a one with lots of activities. According to an expert on aging, the more visitors a nursing home receives—including relatives and members of community organizations—the better the quality of care for the residents, says Karl Pillemer, a sociologist and gerontologist at Cornell University (*Work and Family Life*).

WHEN FAMILY CRISES AND PROBLEMS ARISE...

Many families have a long history of working together on shared problems but many others do not. For some families, the idea of developing and then following through on a plan for collective action is foreign. And it goes without saying that it's harder to become a cohesive problem-solving unit when family members are fragmented by space, time, conflicts and crises. New behavior patterns might be needed in order to deal with a crisis or problem.

When a family is in an uproar and a decision must be made, a family conference is the alternative to one member taking charge and making all the decisions.

5

Medically Speaking

A re you allergic to anything they ask? Well, I'm not sure exactly. I'm pretty sure its my mother who's allergic to penicillin, or is it me? Then more questions. And there you are, sitting and trying to figure out where the heck you are in your cycle so you have some clue as to whether or not you actually could be pregnant again. How about that last pap smear? Hey, did your kids have all their shots? Well, what do you mean all? Out of how many? And, of course, you have no idea exactly which ones they were—or exactly when then had them. Ugh! Really sorry, I don't mean to sound careless but I've had a few hundred things on my mind!

BE PREPARED FOR EMERGENCIES!

During the course of your life as a working Mother, you are bound to be faced with an emergency situation. The key to handling emergencies is being prepared in advance, before the actual emergency. *Baby Talk* magazine offers these guidelines:

    1. Plan which hospital emergency room

you'll use now, before an emergency situation strikes. If your community has a children's hospital or an emergency department specifically geared for children, you may want to make that your emergency destination. Ask you doctor for his or her recommendation and chart the best route between your home and the hospital.

Pediatrician: _____
_____

Hospital/emergency room/phone numbers:
_____
_____

Best route to the hospital: _____
_____
_____
_____

Alternate route: _____
_____
_____
_____

2. Post the number of your local poison control center and the number of your local emergency medical system (if it's something other than "911") next to the telephone. If you think that your child may have been poisoned, call the poison control center first. Keep a bottle of syrup of ipecac in the house to give to your child if the poison control center advises.

Poison control: _____

3. Keep a written record of your child's medical history, including any medications she or he is taking, and bring it with you if you go to the emergency room. Have your medical insurance card and any other necessary paperwork handy, too. If your child has a chronic health problem or is taking several medications, ask your doctor to write all the information down for you. List that information here:

Medical insurance number:

_____

_____

Your child's medical history: _____

_____

_____

4. Before you leave your child with a sitter or relative, be sure to leave a telephone number where you can be reached in an emergency. And write out a parental consent that will allow your child to receive emergency care if he or she has to go into the hospital while you're away. Although a child would not be denied care if the condition were life-threatening, some hospitals might delay treating an injury like a laceration that requires stitches until they can contact you.

STAYING OUT OF THE EMERGENCY ROOM

This year, one in four children will suffer an injury serious enough to require medical attention. Unintentional injuries kill about 8,000 children in the U.S. every year—more than all childhood diseases combined. Many of these injuries can be prevented.

Baby Talk magazine offers the following tips to help parents stay out of the emergency room:

✓ Drowning is the leading cause of unintentional, injury-related death in children ages one through four. Never leave your child unsupervised near water, even for a moment—this includes sinks, bathtubs, toilets and buckets of water.

✓ Burns brought more than 30,000 kids to emergency rooms last year. Because their skin is thinner than an adults, children can sustain a more severe burn in a shorter time. Set your hot-water heater at 120 degrees to prevent scalds, and keep irons, hair dryers, and other small appliances completely out of your child's reach.

✓ Every year, 130 kids are fatally poisoned, and children under four are at the greatest risk. Keep medicines, vitamins, cigarettes (and ashtrays), cosmetics, household cleaners, paints, and pesticides locked up and clearly labeled. Always store hazardous materials in their original containers and rid your house and yard of poisonous plants.

✓ Buckle your child into a car safety seat on every ride.

✓ Choking is another preventable injury. Keep foods that could cause choking—nuts, candies, hard beans—out of reach of children under three, and make sure that your baby can't get at any toys or other objects smaller than 1 and 1/4 inches in diameter.

✓ To prevent cuts and broken bones, never put an infant in a carrier on a high surface. Lots of babies have rocked their carriers over.

✓ Make sure sharp edges and corners are safely padded, and install bars on windows higher than the ground floor. Screens aren't strong enough to keep a child in.

FIRST AID

If you are a parent—even if you're not a parent, that's how important I think this is—I strongly recommend learning CPR (cardio pulmonary resuscitation), infant and child CPR and first aid. It only takes a few hours to become certified and it can really save a life. To find out how you can sign up for classes, contact your local chapter of the American Red Cross.

IMMUNIZATION (THE DREADED SHOTS!)

With all that we working parents have to do, it's hard to keep track of the many responsibilities that we owe to our children. One of the absolute necessities for your child's health is ensuring that he or she has been immunized. According to Dr. Loraine Stern, of *Woman's Day* magazine, "the real danger is failing to have your children fully vaccinated by age two." Dr. Stern reports that less than half of all two year-olds are fully protected. Most children do catch up with their shots by the time they reach kindergarten because shots are required for school entry, but the diseases pose the greatest risk to children under two.

Obtain an immunization schedule from your child's pediatrician at birth and post it on your refrigerator door or another high-visibility location. Discuss the schedule of shots with your doctor or pediatrician or call the Immunization hotline at 800-232-2522.

Of course, when your child does have to go for a shot, *Woman's Day* magazine offers these comfort suggestions:

1. **Be there.** Stay with your child during a shot to soothe and comfort him or her. Praise a child afterward, even if it took six people to give one shot. You can say something like, "I know it was hard for you, and you did really well. What can we do to make it easier next time?"

2. Be honest. Tell a child that the shot may hurt a little and that it's all right to cry.

3. Ask your pediatrician what ways he or she may have to help your child cope with the pain and anxiety, like applying an anesthetic cream before the shot and "blowing the pain away" during the procedure and afterward. To reduce the discomfort of the DTP (diphtheria, tetanus, pertussis shot) give an infant a dose of acetaminophen (children's Tylenol) 30-60 minutes before the inoculation.

4. Stay on schedule. A minor illness such as a cold, an ear infection or diarrhea is no reason to postpone a shot. Doing so may cause your child to fall behind on immunizations. If your child is sick, inform your pediatrician. Children who miss immunizations do not have to start over, they can just pick up where they left off and catch up.

5. Don't let the cost deter you. If your insurance does not cover vaccines, or if you have no insurance and cannot afford the shots, your local public-health service will give them to your child free, although hours may be limited and older children may not be covered. Speak with your pediatrician.

TOUGH TIMES? SPEAK UP!

Many physicians are willing to charge less for their services during tough economic times. If you are quoted a fee that seems too high or is more than you can pay, tell the doctor. Ask if the fee can be lowered or if some other payment plan can be devised (*Bottom Line*).

A good resource to have on hand is *150 Ways to be a Savvy Medical Consumer,* by Charles B. Inlander, President People's Medical Society, 462 Walnut Street, Allentown, Pennsylvania 18102. $5.95.

IS IT A TEASPOON ... OR IS IT A TABLESPOON?

Whenever my daughter gets sick you can bet I've just run out of whatever medicine she needs at the moment—like cough syrup, Tylenol, or Triaminic. I never buy more than one of these at a time because I usually have just enough cash on me to buy the one medicine and a handful of other items I can't go home without. When the medicine runs out, I put the empty bottle on the counter until I remember to write down the name of it in my day book. I eventually throw out the bottle and drag its name through other things-to-do-today lists, until the day (usually about 10 lists later) when I no longer feel like transferring it again. Either I remember one day when I'm in the drugstore buying the toothpaste I'm out of, or I figure it out when it's too late—which brings me back to the beginning of this paragraph....

Now, to keep from that kind of insanity, there are a number of things available to you that can make your life a little easier. First of all, there's probably at least one pharmacy in your area that delivers. If you need medication during off-hours, many pharmacies offer 24-hour service. List the names and numbers of your pharmacy, a pharmacy in your area that delivers and the nearest 24-hour pharmacy:

Pharmacies: _____

_____

_____

Pharmacy that delivers: _____

_____

24-hour pharmacy and convenience store: _____

_____

_____

TOO ILL, OR NOT TOO ILL?

Getting the medication is actually the easy part. What's difficult is deciding whether your child is well enough to attend school and, if not, whether your child is ill enough to require you to stay home with him or her. This is one of those situations where you may need your "emergency people" and their numbers, so look them up now and jot them down here:

_____

_____

_____

OH, NO, NOT TODAY!

DEB*servation:* You can always count on your child getting sick when you have something elaborate planned. It could be the meeting it took weeks to line up, or your most important day at work, or the lunch you've been planing for six months, and on and on.

Many a mother has shoved a child off to school in that "iffy" stage of deciding whether or not the kid is really sick—feeling a little guilty but prepared to launch back home if the worst occurs. We tell ourselves that least we get a couple of hours in—I know it sounds terrible.

Few mothers admit they are annoyed at being inconvenienced by a child's sickness. You're not angry at the child, goodness no!—just ticked off at your own bad luck!

If you really can't stay home with them, be prepared by finding someone who you know is terrific with kids who don't feel well. Save this person for all such "special" occasions.

You really need to back yourself up—especially if there is no way you can't go to work. Barter this care with another mother who may be home during the day and promise to do a "make good" for her some evening. Keep your list of back-ups handy.

Names and phone numbers of people or organizations you can count on:

_____

_____

_____

_____

_____

_____

MEDICAL CLAIMS

As agonizing as an illness or injury can be, waiting for the medical claim to be processed can also be a source of tremendous frustration. *In The Medical Claims Game ... and How to Win It*, G.J. Watkins offers these suggestions:

✓ Write the patient's name and the policy-holder's name on every page of the claim.

✓ Find out how much time you have to file a claim and meet that deadline.

✓ Ask the doctor or hospital to give you an itemized bill listing the diagnostic and/or procedural codes, as well as the charges and dates of all services rendered.

✓ Don't mix different family members on the same claim.

✓ Arrange claims—especially those for pharmacy reimbursements—in chronological order.

✓ Before you mail a claim, make copies of everything.

✓ Don't send your premium in the same envelope as a claim.

A LITTLE EXTRA ADVICE

In this day and age, you can't be too careful. Call the American Board of Medical Specialties, 800-776-CERT, to verify your doctor's certification.

You! You! You!

You are of no help to anyone, including your children, if you are not healthy yourself. So, without further ado:

Your doctor: _____

Date of last visit: _____

Date of next appointment: _____

Gynecologist: _____

Date of last visit: _____

Date of next appointment: _____

Date of last period: _____

Date of last pap smear: _____

Date of last mammography: _____

Specialists: _____

Eye doctor: _____

Date of last eye exam:
_____

Dentist:
_____

Date of last dental appointment:
_____

Date of next appointment:
_____

Your blood type:
_____

Your parent's, in-law's, spouse and kids' blood types:
_____
_____
_____
_____

PMS—IT'S REAL!

So real, in fact, that a woman in England was acquitted of a murder charge by using PMS as her defense! Now before you start making up your hit list, I think a more practical solution in controlling PMS is by learning about it. There are over 150 possible symptoms associated with PMS, both physical and psychological. Psychological symptoms include irritability, depression and anxiety. Physical symptoms include bloating, headaches and fatigue. Each woman suffers different symptoms and to a different extent. Call your doctor or gynecologist, or 800-222-4PMS for a free packet of information about pre-menstrual syndrome and tips for behavior modification that may alleviate these symptoms.

MEN AND PMS—THEY STILL HAVE NO CLUE

If you experience relationship difficulties with your significant other of the opposite sex during a time when you are suffering from PMS, I have discovered a great book about PMS written specifically by a man for men. It's a brief (29 pages including calendars) handbook, written by Frank P. Maimone, called *The Patient Man's Solution to Pre-Menstrual Syndrome: A Practical Guide to Better Relationships.*

Hey, relationships are difficult enough as it is, throw in PMS and you've discovered the recipe for a ticking time bomb. Give your guy a break by ordering him a copy of this book. You wouldn't believe how many guys asked me for a copy after they heard me talk about this on the radio show.

BREAST CANCER

The statistics really blow your mind don't they? One in nine? I'm one of the many women who have fibrocystic disease, meaning there are a million lumps in my breasts. Breast checks are key—the doctor always says I'd be able to tell—but lord knows I have no idea what I'm looking for. I want to learn, and you should too, because breast cancer is serious stuff.

When you make your appointment with your gynecologist and discuss your menstrual cycle, also inform him or her about your concern with breast wellness. Breast cancer is the most commonly diagnosed cancer among women 35 to 54 in the U.S. The American Cancer Society estimates that one in nine women will develop breast cancer during her lifetime. Although that may sound grim, there is good news—if breast cancer is detected early a woman has as much as a 90% chance of survival.

Talk to your doctor about mammograms and being tested for breast cancer, and use the following tips from *Redbook* magazine to conduct a breast self-exam:

1. Standing in front of a mirror, inspect breasts for any changes in contour and nipple shape, and for discharge. Repeat with hands behind head and with hands on hips.

2. In the shower, raise your left arm; move the pads of the three middle fingers of your right hand in small circles, pressing firmly, around the left breast. Start at the other edge and slowly work toward the nipple, covering the entire breast, including your arm and up to your collar bone.

3. Repeat on right side with your left hand. If you do feel a lump check if there is a similar lump on your other breast; it may just be a gland or a rib. See your doctor if you find any abnormalities.

EXERCISE AS A PREVENTATIVE MEASURE

Scientists from the University of Southern California have found that regular exercise cuts the risk of getting breast cancer before menopause. Researchers compared 545 women newly diagnosed with the disease (all age 40 or younger) to an equal number of healthy women matched for age, race, childbirth history and residential neighborhood. Those who exercised one to three hours a week had a 30 percent lower risk of breast cancer. Women who were active for four or more hours fared even better, with a 50 percent lower risk. The physically active women in the study participated in sports such as tennis, swimming, jogging or walking. Some worked out at a gym or attended dance or aerobics classes (*Working Mother* magazine).

BREAST CANCER RESOURCES

As a company that cares about the total well-being of women everywhere, Avon has created the Avon Worldwide Fund of Women's Health. The goal of this global initiative is to improve the health of women around the world. As part of this plan, Avon's Breast Cancer Awareness Crusade was developed to educate women about breast cancer and to provide more women—particularly low-income, minority and older women—with access to early detection services. Through the sales of breast cancer awareness pins and key rings, Avon has raised almost $7 million for community-based breast cancer education and early detection services.

If you need information on breast cancer and early detection services in your area, Avon recommends calling the National Cancer Institute at **800-4-CANCER**. Women with breast cancer who need help and support can call the Y-Me National Breast Cancer Organization at 800 221-2141. Your call will be completely confidential.

Mental Health—In My Case, A Lost Cause

How about the fact that now that I'm getting older I'm sure I'm dying of everything ... the allergic reaction ... the raspy throat ... the chest pain that turns out to be indigestion ... good news there are hotline numbers for nuts like me ... an impartial and informative answer to what the deal is before I leave and drive myself to the emergency room. Think I'm kidding? I've been there plenty of times ... primarily for the panic attacks—which really give you a run for your money in the life-and-death department.

Mental health problems can be just as crippling as physical problems. While it's socially acceptable to receive treatment for a physical ailment, there seems to be a stigma attached to receiving help for a mental disorder. In her column in *Good Housekeeping*, Dr. Joyce Brothers writes that nearly half of all Americans have had a mental problem that could have been helped by counseling—but only one in four sought help. "Counseling,"

Dr. Brothers writes, "is not just a last resort in a crisis; it can enrich your life. Don't be afraid to consider it."

MENTAL HEALTH RESOURCES

The National Mental Health Association can offer you brochures on stress, depression, schizophrenia and other mental health problems along with a list of local associations and referrals. Call 800-969-6642, Monday through Friday, 9 a.m. to 5 p.m.

DEB*news:*
If you need more immediate, "round-the-clock" phone counseling, you can call **1-900-THERAPY**.
As part of the San Francisco-based Summit Solutions Line, a team of 300 therapists from around the country are available to help anyone who reaches out to them.
Each call is $3.99 per minute.

PANIC ATTACKS (NO, YOU'RE NOT DYING!)

During my career as a radio talk show host, I have come across some startling information about anxiety disorders. According to the National Institute of Mental Health, they are the most common of all psychiatric disorders and affect more than 23 million Americans, 13% of the population.

A common manifestation of anxiety disorder is panic attacks. If you suffer from an anxiety or panic disorder you may feel the following symptoms: sweating, shortness of breath, pounding of the heart, tightness in the chest, shakiness, feeling of choking, tingling, hot or cold flashes, faintness, trembling and nausea.

Because the symptoms can mimic those associated with various heart abnormalities, thyroid problems or respiratory problems, panic patients often fear they are dying, about to faint, or about to have a stroke. Discuss the symptoms with your doctor. Your ailment, whether physical or mental, is debilitating and your doctor can help you.

If you discover that your symptoms are related to an anxiety disorder, Jerilyn Ross, in her book *Triumph Over Fear*, has some suggestions to ease your anxiety and fear. When you are in a stressful situation and feel that you may become panic-stricken, Ross outlines the following points:

✓ Expect, allow and accept that fear will rise.
✓ When fear comes, stop, wait and let it be.
✓ Focus on and do manageable things in the present.
✓ Label your level of fear from 0-10. Watch it go up and down.
✓ Function with fear. Appreciate your achievements.
✓ Expect, allow and accept that fear will reappear.

PLAIN OL' BLUES

Clinical depression is a very serious illness that demands immediate and intensive intervention. But even being "down in the dumps" can be debilitating. If you find yourself in a funk, avoid venting your feelings by crying or shouting, spending time alone or blaming your problems on others.

A study conducted by Dr. Randy Larsen, Ph.D., associate professor of psychology at the University of Michigan, has found that these common coping strategies don't work and may, in fact, prolong and worsen the sad feelings. Larsen speculates that taking an active approach works better. His study identified seven effective ways to cheer yourself up:

1. Take some action to solve your problem.
2. See the good as well as the bad in your situation.
3. Compare your troubles to other people's problems to get perspective.
4. Compare your latest crisis to previous troubles you've mastered.
5. Think about past successes you've had.
6. Reward yourself in some special way.
7. Resolve to try harder in the future to avoid problems like the one that made you blue.

THE ALL TOO COMMON COLD

As Moms, we know we don't have time to be sick—even if our ailment is just a cold. Now, if you practice "wellness," you can reduce the risk of catching a cold by:

✓ Taking a multi-vitamin. As many as 15% of healthy American women may have mild nutrient deficiencies that could weaken their immunity. While eating right is the best move, try a muli-vitamin and mineral supplement once a week.

✓ Avoid stress. There's evidence that people under stress have twice the risk of getting colds as calmer people do. To stay healthy, try adjusting your attitude. Studies show that people who see demands as a challenge, rather than as a burden, are less likely to get sick.

✓ Wash your hands often. Cold and flu germs can be transmitted by touch. Wash your hands if you've been around a sick person. Keep unwashed fingers away from your eyes, mouth and nose, where germs can enter the body (*McCall's*).

6

❧✦❧

Money Matters—
It Really Does

Money? Oh, yeah, that crinkley green stuff that evaporates out of my wallet ... or out of my bra where I sometimes keep it when I just can't deal with trying to find my wallet in my pocketbook! Oh, and cash machines: incredible phenomena ... the touchy-feely screens, secret codes and yes, cash is available. There's the sound of the engine gearing up with more money!

However, there are times when you have money—and it's just NOT available. Thank goodness I made friends at the bank. They've kept me from losing a whole bunch of friends in real life.

Why? Because everybody always owes me money exactly when I need to pay money to everybody else. It's no fun standing there in the serious area of the bank begging my banker friends to cover checks on promised checks to me that should have been in yesterday. But, if you've taken the time to get to know the people in the bank, the begging actually works, and this will get you by, at least until the next time....

CREDIT CARDS

Just for a minute, every once in a while, I feel like I'm loaded and credit cards do the trick! God I hate to pay those things back, though. They got me into a real jam once, too. Here's the lesson I learned: Never, never use credit card money to front a business ... like, in case, the business doesn't work and you're left with the debt ... and then those people who are hired to act like TELEPHONE HIT MEN call you with those 800 numbers attached to their names and you start hiding from them like a fugitive. And isn't it great when these people call you at work, and leave all those messages, so that anybody who may have once thought you were an upstanding citizen now thinks you're a deadbeat? Except how do THEY know what the 800 means, if they haven't been there themselves?

Anyway, to keep you from getting into jams like mine, better keep this information handy:

Your bank(s) _____

_____

Phone number(s) _____

Savings account number _____

Checking account number _____

Toll-free numbers for your credit cards

_____

_____

_____

The numbers to call to cancel your cards when
lost or stolen:

_____

_____

_____

DEB*fact:*
Sixty percent of American adults have
at least one credit card, and on
average owes $2, 317!

Money is always a problem, especially if you have kids.
If you think those credit card people are rough, how
about your kid when the tooth fairy is cheaper than
usual. (Just so you know, the going rate is $1.75 per
tooth, according to the *Wall Street Journal,* up from $1 in
1990.). Or how about when your kid absolutely, positively
needs (not wants, but needs) to have those super-duper,
air-pumped, six-million-dollar man, bionic sneakers. A
parent can go insane!

MONEY TOPS SEX!

Money is the number one reason couples argue. More than a third of American women between 18 and 64 think having enough money is more important than good sex to the success of the marriage. Money has become sexier than sex! I recently read in *USA Today* that, on an average day, more people in the U.S. are thinking about money than about sex! Well, in light of what I just said, skip my chapter on romance, dim the lights, pop the bottle of champagne, light the candles and talk dollars and cents. That may be the best (and safest) romance you encounter. The worst case scenario is you end up with all the lights back on and in separate rooms.

But seriously, how are you going to make ends meet? What's the best way to stretch that paycheck? The first step in managing your money is making sure that both spouses are involved in money matters. If you're not already involved with the family's finances, you should become involved, for two reasons. First, it's likely that, at some point in your life, you will have to deal with the family finances. Esther Berger, a senior vice president for Paine Webber and author of *Money Smart: Secrets Women Need to Know About Money,* reports that 48% of all married women will be widowed, and 36% will be divorced during their lifetimes. So you're better off becoming prepared with finances now. Don't wait until you're forced to manage the family money.

Secondly, kids learn about money primarily from their parents. Show your kids that you understand how money works and that you will stand up for yourself in financial matters.

Child Magazine, in an article entitled, "What Every Mom Needs to Know About Money," recommends that if you are not involved in the family's finances, you should:

✓ Enlist your husband's support. Tell him that, for the family's sake, you'd like to know more about money matters and need to know what to do in an emergency.

✓ Suggest a monthly meeting. Going through the bills together once a month can be a good starting point.

✓ Maintain a sense of cooperation. Set aside emotionally charged issues, such as who spends more, during money sessions. Focus on making the most of the money you have.

PEACE OF MIND

Child Magazine also recommends you get organized. There's peace of mind in knowing where to find your tax records and financial documents. If you haven't organized your documents, you might want to set up files in the following categories:

✓ Property documents—Copies of your mortgage deed and other proof of real estate ownership; title to cars and boats, list of insured goods and furnishings.

✓ Investment and debt records—Include paperwork relating to your stocks and bonds (including your broker's name and original stock prices), loans, credit cards, checking accounts, IRAs and 401(k) plans.

✓ Insurance—Include policies, receipts, claims papers and settlement records.

✓ Tax records—Keep past federal and state income tax returns, and all statements of income. If you itemize your deductions, keep all supporting receipts and documents.

✓ Credit rating—It's also important to check your credit rating. Keeping your credit rating free of errors is really crucial because "your credit rating is a reflection of who you are as a financial person," says Berger. To check your credit report for accuracy, request a copy from the TRW Corp. (800-422-4879), one of the three major credit reporting agencies and the only one to offer a free report each year.

GET YOUR OWN CREDIT!

If you haven't done so already, it's important to establish your own credit. The Equal Credit Opportunity Act of 1977 requires that joint accounts, used by husband and wife, be reported in both names. This means that, for better or worse, you share your husband's credit rating and you and your spouse are responsible for all debts and charges. You should have at least one credit account in your own name, so you can establish your own credit identity and history.

It's smart to set up a savings account or investment account in your own name, too. If you're a stay-at-home mom, it's important for you to have a security blanket. Even if you only tuck away a few dollars each month, you are doing something important for yourself. And sooner or later, it will grow into sum sizable enough to invest in a place other than a bank.

If we're learning about finances, we might as well learn a little something about investment while we're at it. There's a great book called *99 Great Answers to Everyone's Investment Questions* by Linda Bryant, Diane Pearl and Ellie Williams. They say that when you consider any kind of investment, there are several questions you should ask, including:

> ✓ How does this investment make its money? (A stock means you become part-owner of the company; a bond means you are paid interest on the money you lend.)
> ✓ When will my original investment be returned? Is there a date before which you can't get your money without paying a penalty?

MONEY FOR COLLEGE? IT'S ON THE HOUSE

Investing in your home may make more sense than traditional saving for the kids college tuition, or your own retirement. Financial consultant Stephen Pollan says the formula to keep in mind is this: If the child is less than 10 years old, and you are under age 50, money spent on renovations that increase your home's value may be worth more in the long run than participation in a college or retirement savings plan.

When the time comes for college or retirement, you can borrow against the home to pay for them. You will have increased the home's value and your equity in it through the renovations.

PAY THE ELECTRONIC WAY

Something that's made my life easier is my bank's telephone service line. I call up, punch in my account number, and the service line will tell me how much I have left in my checking account, and which checks have cleared and which are outstanding. This keeps me sane (or insane, depending on what my balance is!).

Newer banking services allow you to pay bills whose balances change each month, like credit cards and utility bills. This can be done any number of ways, by using your ATM card, a touch tone telephone, personal computer and even your TV.

HOW IT WORKS

First you must "enroll" with your bank by completing an authorization form that lists each company you regularly pay. Once you set this up, funds are either transferred electronically between your account and the merchants. For those businesses not equipped to receive electronic payments, a paper check is issued. These payments appear on your monthly bank statement.

If you want to pay bills using your personal computer, you'll need to get a modem and special software. Two software companies that offer payment programs are Checkfree (800-882-5280) and Prodigy (800-776-3449). Just remember these services charge a fee which can vary from $120 to $3000 a year. Some banks offer similar services. Charges vary by bank.

There is also a way to pay via your television. Called Interactive TV services, this electronic bill-paying system is offered by the Eon Corp. (703-715-8600). The system uses a VCR size device that hooks up to your TV and is remote controlled (*Good Housekeeping*).

TO KEEP OUT OF TROUBLE WITH CREDITORS

✓ Make small payments on each bill. Avoid the practice of paying some in full while ignoring others altogether.

✓ Stick to your revised payment plan. If you've promised to pay only $250 on your mortgage, say, stick to that plan.

✓ Draw up a payment schedule. Pay your rent first! But don't let other bills go unpaid for long.

✓ Compare interest rates, grace periods, etc., this way you can organize payments so that you pay a minimum in fees.

✓ Don't avoid creditors. Explain the problem and ask if you can stretch out payments (*Family Circle*).

DEB*note:*

How often do American families worry they
won't be able to pay their bills?
(Actually, this surprised me—I thought more
people were
getting gray over this!)

All the time—10%
Most of the time—10%
Some of the time—33%
Almost never/never—47%

7

Food, Glorious Food

Food is my favorite sport. Not much of it tastes bad to me, and there's not much of it I haven't worn, meaning simply that I'm a spiller/stainer. It comes with always being in a rush. I eat in my car because nothing makes a ride go by faster than food and coffee; I eat on the train, at my desk, on the couch, and I'll eat in bed if need be. Of course, dining out is really my favorite, because somebody else clears the table and does the dishes. And the pots. Boy, do I hate doing pots. The worst thing in the world is when you're stupid enough to leave them till the morning.

Oh, and lately I've developed "chicken phobia." I wash the counter 25 times after I clean chicken for fear of salmonella poisoning, and then continue to wonder throughout dinner if I, in fact, did touch the lettuce "accidentally."

Oh, too, I've become quite proficient at performing my weekly food funeral, which goes something like this:

There I am, refrigerator door swung open with my head inside, staring. I'm starving, irrational, tired and not in the mood for anything—surely not anything in THIS refrigerator, which is odd because when I shopped for the stuff my mind was full of possibilities. In fact, I was thrilled by the elaborate uses I could make of each thing I lugged home. I saw chicken in the poultry case and thought, Chicken Marsala! Why not? I've got a jar of mushrooms at home, and while I'm not exactly sure how to make the sauce brown, I'll figure it out. In the produce section I saw vegetables and thought, fresh salads! And carrot and celery sticks available everyday chopped fresh. I see fresh tomato salads with olive oil and Italian bread. I see three-bean salads, a regular protein carnival ... and fresh Ricotta cheese to top off the homemade gravy (sauce for you non-Italians) for the penne. I had all these wonderfully inspired plans, but somehow ... oh well, it's time, once again, for the food funeral.

ORGAN MUSIC, PLEASE ...

Start the dreary organ music, please. Good-bye yogurt, you expired three days earlier and I never had a chance to say farewell. Next comes the poor Ricotta ... I shoulda never opened it and used only half, but who knew? Hmmm, the date on this meat says ... oh darn, just missed it! Hello lettuce, you shriveled green thing, you. Sorry we never bonded. Now here, here I'm truly shocked ... I thought lemons lived forever. Oh, fresh seal bologna, I knew I should've pressed harder on the seal. An unidentified leftover (I think it was the extra tuna that didn't make it into the sandwich) is being saved under a tinfoil tent in food purgatory, which means I must have at some point judged it to be not quite dead enough to throw away, but now I must reverse that decision because no one is ever going to actually eat the thing, which is the best and final test. So now it joins the funeral procession into the big plastic garbage bag. Great, now I can order Chinese food!

How many nights a week does your family eat together? Compare yourself with the national average based on results from a poll conducted by *Parenting* magazine.

> Every night of the week—35%
> Five to six nights—33%
> Three to four nights—20%
> Zero to two nights—11%

A HALF-DOZEN DEBTIPS:

1. Eliminate odors in a refrigerator or freezer with ordinary charcoal briquettes. Place two or three in each compartment. Replace monthly, returning the "used" ones to the bag to be burned on the grill (*The Tightwad Gazette*).

2. No spurt drinks. The next time you or your kids open a drink box, hold it by the two narrow sides when pushing in the straw. This prevents juice from spurting out, which often happens when you hold the box front and back (*Good Housekeeping*).

3. Eat a lot of fish. Chances are you're "fish deficient." On average, Americans eat a half an ounce of fish a day, about one bite's worth. Just doubling that amount could do wonders for your heart. Fish is one food where fattier is healthier. The unique oil in fish, omega-3 fatty acids, thins the blood, which thwarts the clogging that can trigger heart attacks and strokes. Fish oil also lowers blood pressure and triglycerides (potentially dangerous blood fat), raises levels of good HDL (high density lipoproteins) cholesterol, regulates the heartbeat and helps block processes that promote arthritis and cancer. Best catches: mackerel, herring, sardines, salmon, tuna, turbot, bass, bluefish, swordfish and trout. Fresh, frozen or canned, these fish have the most good fat (*USA Weekend*).

4. Salted water takes longer to boil, so always bring the water to a boil before adding salt! (*Dinner in Minutes: Memorable Meals for Busy Cooks*, by Linda Gassenheimer).

5. If you don't like the smell of cooking broccoli, brussel sprouts or cauliflower, throw a couple chunks of bread or pieces of red pepper into the cooking water . Use a slotted spoon to retrieve the pot sweeteners before serving (*The Food Lover's Tiptionary*).

6. Love eating garlic but hate the aftertaste and odor? Try chewing a couple fennel seeds, a coffee bean, or munch on some fresh parsley.

Drinking lemon juice mixed with a little sugar or eating lime sherbet will do the trick, too (*The Food Lover's Tiptionary*).

FOODS THAT HEAL

Research has found links between health and certain foods. Here's the lowdown:

Almonds fight heart disease
Avocados are good for cholesterol
Garlic may lift your mood
Celery may lower your blood pressure
Broccoli helps fight cancer
Hot peppers relieve congestion
Spinach reduces risk of cataracts
Wheat bran may deter colon cancer
Cinnamon is good for blood sugar
Beans cut cholesterol
Cranberries fight bladder infections
Cloves and cumin are antioxidants
Cabbage discourages breast cancer
Soybeans offer anti-cancer elements
Red wine and grape juice keep blood thin
Licorice soothes ulcers
Ginger prevents nausea and motion sickness
Yogurt boosts immunity
Honey helps put you to sleep
Chicken soup really does relieve colds
Onions and apples promote longevity
(*USA Weekend*)

TEN ILLNESS-FIGHTING FOODS FOR KIDS:

✓ Peanut butter is an excellent source of monounsaturated fat, the kind that helps protect against heart disease because it lowers the 'bad' cholesterol levels in the blood and increases the good cholesterol.

✓ Apples—a great source of soluble fiber that helps prevent heart disease.

✓ Kiwifruit —ounce for ounce, it has more Vitamin C than almost any fruit, which research suggests may lessen cold symptoms.

✓ Sweet potatoes—the Vitamin A in sweet potatoes comes in the form of beta carotene. Giving your child just a half sweet potato dishes up more than the RDA for Vitamin A and about 25% RDA for Vitamin C.

✓ Broccoli—contains cancer-fighting substances called Flavenoids, and is a good source of beta carotene and Vitamin C.

✓ Lean red meat—lean beef, lamb, pork, and veal are among the best sources of the essential minerals iron and zinc. A shortage of iron can lead to irritability, fatigue and a decrease in attention span. Zinc helps normal growth and development of the immune system.

✓ Fortified cereal—iron-fortified breakfast cereals have helped reduce anemia in kids, and cereal with milk supplies vitamin A for eyesight, growth and strong immune systems, and B vitamins needed to get energy from food.

✓ Legumes—rich in protein and iron, they have less saturated fat and cholesterol than meat or poultry. Kidney beans, lima beans, and other legumes are packed with the two types of fiber that protect against heart disease, diabetes and cancer.

✓ Yogurt—a great source of calcium to build strong bones and protect against osteoporosis. Also, bacteria cultures in yogurt may boost immunity against certain stomach and intestinal viral infections. Yogurt also replenishes the bacteria in your child's intestinal tract after diarrhea or antibiotics.

✓ Wheat germ—a good source of Vitamin E, folic acid, and zinc. Vitamin E, another antioxidant, has been linked to heart health and to a strong immune system. Kids need folic acid for healthy blood cells and zinc for growth (*Child* magazine).

LOOKING TO GET PICKED UP IN THE AFTERNOON?

When you need a nutrition boost, and a jolt of energy that lasts, try a nutritious low-fat snack loaded with fast-acting carbohydrates, vitamins and minerals: Tops on the list are:

Fresh fruit
Low fat tortillas
Fresh veggies
Low fat milk
Fruit juices (no sugar added)

Pretzels
Raisins
Air popped popcorn
Rice cakes
Low fat yogurt
Bagels
Low fat pudding
Low fat crackers

Add a little aerobic activity to these snacks and you'll have energy to spare (*Healthy Nutrition News*).

Your List:

Supermarkets that deliver: _____

_____

_____

Restaurants that deliver: _____

_____

_____

Favorite restaurants for business: _____

_____

Favorite restaurants for pleasure: _____

_____

_____

Name of the last great bottle(s) of wine you had (if you don't write down, you'll never remember!):

_____

_____

Last but not least, here's a place for the shopping lists that are always left at home on the kitchen counter:

Shopping list:

_____

_____

_____

_____

_____

_____

_____

_____

_____

_____

_____

_____

_____

_____

8

Car Things

You haven't lived until you've had your car booted for not paying parking tickets. Booted, for those of you who may not have ever experienced this pleasure, is when the local police department affixes a large neon orange metal object to your tire to lock the wheel in place so you cannot drive the vehicle. If this is not enough, they also slap an unremovable sticky sign on your driver side window. Anybody who may have missed the neon orange metal object will then have eye-level evidence that you're a moron.

Now it's not like I don't want to pay these parking tickets—I have mailed in a few on time before they quadrupled—but they sort of get put aside: on the counter, in various pocketbooks, on the dashboard, over the visor. They're out of sight until the last possible moment of truth has arrived, which for me is going to court and pleading insanity to a judge to get the fine lowered.

Sometimes, if you get enough of these tickets, you get your registration or license revoked. Needless to say, you can't renew either one until you pay up, with money that you don't have—money that you could have spent on something nice instead. Anyway, you promise this will never happen again.

As I sit here writing this chapter my car is booted in

front of a parking meter in the town near my home. Why? I don't know. I actually did pay some of the tickets and they couldn't have possibly added up so fast. You see, there's nowhere to park in this town filled with two-hour meters for my 12-hour days! There's a waiting list for permit parking at the train station that's three- years long and the taxis back and forth add up to a small fortune. Besides, when I drop my daughter off at school and run a few errands, I am not going back home to re-park the car and call a cab. So, I take my chances. I stuff as much money in the meter as possible and hope for the best!

Last night, I get off the train, I'm in heels, carrying a thousand pounds of stuff and I'm supposed to drive my friend home—that is, after I pick up my daughter at a play date. But, no, that's not how it went. The car is "booted," so I walk to the police station. The clerk won't be in until the morning. So I call a taxi so that I can pick up my daughter, drop off my friend, and then go home and scream. I give my baby-sitter a check to bring to the town clerk the next morning to clear up the matter but they don't take checks so I have to call the town clerk and plead insanity, which, of course, is not too far from the truth at this point.

The moral of the story is: pay your tickets. And I will, too, just as soon as I find those two from last month ... I know they're in this car somewhere....

BEST CARS FOR A WOMAN AND HER FAMILY

The Buick LeSabre and the Ford Explorer were named the 1994 *Family Circle* family cars of the year in the two new categories: "family sedan" and "family activity vehicle." They were selected through an independent survey of women who were the principal drivers of cars bought by families (no kidding!). The cars were rated on performance and handling, safety, dependability and reliability, appearance and styling, space and comfort, satisfaction with dealer, value for the money, and suitability for intended uses.

DEB*choice:*

Personally, I love a Jeep. Why? It's fun to drive, I'm up high and look down at everybody. Plus I have tons of room for the endless stuff I find in my possession like tennis racquets, roller blades, clothes for the cleaners, tailors, salvation army, and I can leave them there. It's like having a rolling closet. Most exciting of all, I can go anywhere without worrying about the weather—the four-wheel drive keeps you from being trapped anywhere!

THERE'S NO SUCH THING AS A COOL CAR

✓ Never leave children or animals locked in a closed car, even for a brief time with the windows rolled down a bit. In summer, or summerlike climates, a car's interior temperature can rise to 120 degrees within 15 minutes.

✓ Keep a one-gallon container of water in your trunk for emergencies.

✓ If the engine is steaming turn on the car's emergency flashers and pull over to the side or shoulder of the road.

✓ Never unscrew the radiator cap when the engine is overheated. Wait for it to cool—about 30 minutes—and use a towel or cloth to unscrew the cap. Remember to turn your face away to avoid any escaping steam. Then add water as needed, to the radiator, replace the cap and close it tightly.

✓ If your car has an air-cooled engine, simply pull off the road and allow the engine to cool down—about 30 minutes. Then stop at the next service station to have your car checked for the cause of the overheating (*Family Circle's Hints, Tips and Smart Advice*).

THE PILL FOR YOUR CAR?

That's what it's called, "The Pill"—and it's a highly effective fuel conditioner in a tablet. It's non-corrosive and it works with regular and premium gasoline and even with diesel. Just drop it in your tank when you fill up. The Pill actually cleans a car's engine, increases power, improves mileage, and reduces exhaust emissions by 30% to more than 40%! Guaranteed! The Pill is made from an additive that has been proving itself in heavy-duty industrial applications for 20 years.

The Pill has been sold almost exclusively on QVC, but

you can obtain it by writing to Brian Benlifer, Benlifer Communications, 8 Glen Drive, South Salem, NY, 10590.

KIDS TAXI

Kids Kab, a chain founded by Pam Henderson of Troy, Michigan, is a driving service that picks up kids and deposits them at soccer practice, or wherever they're supposed to be while Mom is at her job. The chain now has 25 franchises in 11 states, but there are lots of local operators too. Phyliss Eggert and Beverly Braton run their service, Kids Wheels, in Denver, Colorado. Parents usually contract for these services on a monthly or yearly basis. Fares range from $5 to $8 per one-way trip. If the service is on its toes, kids should be required to buckle up and to identify themselves with a special photo card. Similar services exist in New York and California, among others (*Woman's Day*).

IMPORTANT CAR INFO TO KEEP HANDY

Your List:

Car license plate numbers:

1) _____

2) _____

3) _____

4) _____

Date driver's license expires:

_____

Date registration(s) expire: _____

_____

Inspection(s) due: _____

Name of auto insurance company and policy
numbers: _____

_____

Date policy (policies) expire: _____

Mechanic's phone number: _____

Date of last service/maintenance and what was
repaired/replaced (you'll never remember this
the next time!): _____

_____

Car service /taxi numbers: _____

_____

Who you can call if you're stuck: _____

_____

_____

_____

9

Travel

*"There is no such thing as
fun for the whole family."*

—JERRY SEINFELD

There's nothing worse than a "list-less" traveler.
At the top of your list make sure you have all
your frequent flyer numbers, 800 numbers for
all the airlines, the names of female-friendly hotels, your
travel agent's number, and all the family vacation ideas
you've been accumulating. Then there's the before-you-
leave-town list and the emergency information list that
you leave with some responsible person you know.

The other day, when I took a swig of mouthwash and
walked away from the sink forgetting to spit it out, I knew
I was in desperate need of a vacation. When I thought
about it, I realized it had been five solid years since my
last official vacation, and that I was probably down to my
last brain cell. There have been a couple of business trips
that afforded me a few hours of reprieve, but not the
real thing.

I started fantasizing about being on a beach somewhere with an exotic colored drink in my hand and head-

phones on with something other than my own thoughts whipping around in my head. But then my daughter comes into the room, and I realize I can't justify leaving her behind. I already feel badly enough about all the time I spend away from her while working.

Then it hit me—Camp Hyatt! When I took my daughter with me on a business trip to Orlando, I checked her into Camp Hyatt, not knowing what to expect. When I picked her up later that day, I knew I'd done the right thing—she loved it so much she didn't want to come back to the room. She had her own little vacation away from me, which I'm sure she needed.

Even better than Orlando was the Hyatt Regency Cerromar in Dorado Beach, Puerto Rico. My daughter begged me to get her to Camp Hyatt early so she could have as much time there as possible. As much as she loved the place, I still felt guilty about not spending the whole day with her. But I managed to keep myself busy with rum punches and sun angling and walking on the beach and ordering turkey kabobs and floating down the world's longest pool and just hanging out with Jeff and popping into the casino in the middle of the day for a couple of minutes and popping back out into the sun—you get the picture!

If Camp Hyatt sounds right for you and yours, call 800-233-1234 for more information.

Phone numbers of other favorite places: _____

_____

_____

_____

_____

_____

_____

CLUB MOM

If you don't have the time for a real vacation, but are in desperate need of a reprieve, I have the perfect weekend place for you! "Club Mom" is a resort in historic Rhode Island FOR MOMS ONLY! Commiserate with other Moms while enjoying a manicure, pedicure or massage. You can also tour the mansions of Newport and enjoy a harbor cruise. For more information, call Jean Paulantonio at 401-624-9138.

TRAVELING SMART

Travel experts Paul Lasley and Elizabeth Harryman have the following advice to offer on traveling smart:

✓ Consult a travel agent, he or she has access to a wealth of information and will be able to tell you about special discounts for airlines, hotels, car rentals, cruises and much more. Take advantage of their expertise.

✓ Always prepare a budget. Calculate the costs of hotels, meals and transportation ahead of time. Don't forget to include such expenses as tips, taxis, newspapers and snacks.

✓ Bring the basics—fine jewelry, expensive watches and high price leather goods will attract unwanted attention. It's best to leave them at home.

✓ Less is more. Most hotels will gladly provide a hair dryer or clothes iron. For long journeys, pack washable fabrics that will dry overnight. If headed to cool climates, take lightweight, thermal underwear for layering, wear slacks and low-heeled shoes on planes and trains for safety, as well as comfort.

✓ "Carry on" is in. Avoid the inconvenience of long lines at baggage claim by packing light and storing luggage on board. If traveling with extra suitcases, pack toiletries, medicine, important papers and a change of clothing in a carry-on bag.

✓ Label everything ... each piece of luggage should be labeled properly inside and out. However, don't use a home address on the luggage tag, use a post office box or work address.

For more information on traveling smart, call American Express 800-221-7282 .

TRAVELER CHECKLIST

✓ Tickets
✓ Passport or birth certificate (if traveling outside the country)
✓ Appointment calendar

✓ Address book
✓ Travelers checks, cash, credit cards
✓ Important papers
✓ Small flashlight
✓ Eyeshades and ear plugs
✓ Antiseptic towelettes
✓ Saline solution
✓ Toiletries
✓ Medications
✓ Foreign phrase book
✓ Small bottle of water
✓ Nuts, raisins or other healthful snacks
✓ Business cards

IMPORTANT INFORMATION TO LEAVE BEHIND

✓ Flight information/itinerary
✓ Phone numbers where you can be reached

If you are leaving kids at home, make sure you leave:

✓ Schedules for their routines
✓ Names and numbers of back-up sitters
✓ Names and numbers of relatives/friends
✓ All medical information
✓ Signed power of attorney forms for
   emergency medical treatment and travel

10

Safety

I used to walk around with that neon sign on my forehead that flashed "mug me, mug me"—until the day came when I actually got mugged! Yup, there I was being marched along by a man who said he had a gun and wanted all my money and jewelry, which I instantly handed over. Fortunately, I wasn't harmed, but I do remember vividly that my whole mind going blank from the panic I felt.

The best advice I can give about safety is that it's up to you to be aware and prepared when it comes to the safety of you and your kids. The best tactic is prevention—stay out of danger's way the best you can. This is not always possible, but simply being safety-minded will decrease the likelihood of being assaulted.

DON'T PANIC

Panic and fear are perfectly natural responses. However, mentally preparing yourself for the reality that you could someday find yourself in an assault situation, and imagining what options you might have can help to decrease the trauma and allow you to react more effectively. Panic, on the other hand, prevents us from recognizing solutions to emergency situations. According to Nancy Hightshoe, former commissioned police officer, safety expert, corporate trainer, and counselor to victims of serious crimes, it makes good safety sense to follow these tips:

✓ If you get an "uh-oh" feeling in your stomach, trust your instincts—there probably is something wrong.

✓ Think like a cop—look at the world like a puzzle and see what doesn't fit.

✓ ATMs—don't use these in unpopulated areas and never at night if you can help it.

✓ When traveling on a bus or subway, don't sit near the door.

✓ If using a rental car, check the equipment on the car so you know how everything works, know where you're going and don't be seen fumbling with a map.

✓ Whether parking at night or in a garage, park as close to the door as possible and try to walk in a well-lit area.

✓ When you walk, walk in the direction of oncoming traffic. Always carry emergency notification information with you and try to vary your schedule or route so you're not a predictable target.

✓ When you go out, leave a talk radio station on in the house.

✓ Teach your children to like the police.

✓ "Come help me find my puppy," is the most popular way kidnappers and child molesters try to lure a kid to go off with them. Role play with your children and teach them how to react in a situation like this.

✓ Being with another person reduces your chances of being a victim by about 60%. This holds true for kids too.

✓ The most sensible safety device you should carry is a shriek alarm.

✓ When traveling, use luggage tags that close so no one sees your address and knows you're out of town. Use a post office address or your business address on the tags.

✓ While lodging in a hotel or motel, don't go out in the hallways alone searching for ice or soda in the middle of the night (Nancy Hightshoe Seminars, P.O. Box 11846, St. Louis, MO 63105-0646).

TWO MUST-HAVE VIDEOS

Out of Harm's Way is a personal safety videotape designed for business people, particularly those who travel, as well as for family members. This tape is especially effective for parents, grandparents and other caring friends to teach children safe habits. $12.50.

Preventing the Reality of Rape is a personal safety videotape program focusing on effective strategies from both the psychological and behavioral perspectives.

Includes 12 commonly held myths about rape as well as the truth about these statements. Both videotapes are available through Nancy Hightshoe Seminars, P.O. Box 11846, St. Louis, MO 63105-0646.

DEB*alert*

If you're driving and you think you are in trouble drive to a police department, fire department or hospital emergency entrance, there's always someone there who can help you.

CRIME BUSTER TIPS FOR HOME SAFETY

A 1993 report by the National Burglar and Fire Alarm Association showed that a home protected by an alarm is three times less likely to be burglarized than a home without one. However, whether or not you have an alarm, here are some crime-buster tips to improve the safety of your home:

✓ Exterior doors should be made of solid wood or metal and fit snugly in their frames. Install deadbolt locks and peepholes.

✓ Door safety chains break easily so don't rely on them for serious protection.

✓ Jam the track of sliding glass doors with a thick wooden dowel.

✓ Prune shrubs so your house is visible from

the street. Cut back all tree branches that provide access to upper-level windows and branches
that droop to the ground that could create a
hiding place for a prowler.

✓ Maintain your lawn so your property looks
occupied.

✓ Position entrance lights to illuminate a
broad area, leaving no dark corners where a
burglar can hide.

✓ Get a barking dog—security experts still
consider a dog one of the best defenses against
intruders.

✓ Join your neighborhood watch association.

CAR SAFETY

According to the FBI, thieves made off with over one
and a half million automobiles in 1992. You can do one
of four things to try to keep your car from becoming one
of the statistics:

✓ Serial numbers etched into glass
✓ A steering wheel lock
✓ An alarm
✓ An immobilization system.

A less expensive option is having the serial number
etched into your front windshield and passenger windows. Most glass shops will do this for about $20.
("Crimebusters, What Works and What Doesn't," excerpt-
ed from an article in *Family Circle*.)

KID SAFETY

Food

✓ Young children should never be allowed to eat unattended. You'll never know if they are choking if you're not there—and it only takes a second for a child to choke.

✓ Children should not eat in the car if its moving. You are not in a position to assist them.

✓ Microwave ovens do not heat evenly so never give children food, especially liquids, that have been heated in a microwave without first testing to see if it's too hot.

Automobile

✓ Always have children in car seats.

✓ Even if you think it will be a quick stop, never leave a child in the car unattended.

✓ To help prevent accidents, have children put their hands on their laps before you close car doors.

Home

✓ A small child can easily drown in an open toilet. They should be closed as well as the bathroom itself.

✓ The same holds true for buckets or any container with even as a little as a few inches of water in it. This is extremely dangerous for a crawling baby who is naturally top heavy and can't pull itself out.

✓ Don't let children bathe by themselves. Put a phone in the bathroom so you won't have to leave for any reason.

✓ Never leave hair blowers or other electrical appliances that are plugged in around sinks.

General

✓ Don't discount the things your children tell you about other adults. Check everything out just to be sure.

✓ Make your children know that talking to strangers is not permitted.

✓ Teach your children not to be taken in by strangers offering gifts or engaging them in conversation. Teach your children what to do if a stranger does approach them.

✓ Never leave children, especially babies unattended with any dog or cat. Children antagonize them and animals instinctively strike back.

Day Care

✓ One of the most common threats that your child faces in a day-care situation is being bitten by other children. Ask your child if this has happened to him or her, you may be surprised at what you find out.

✓ You must make sure that your policy concerning discipline is adhered to by the day-care center. For example, if you are against spanking or other physical abuse as a form of discipline, make sure the day-care center knows that is NOT acceptable or tolerable.

✓ What kind of screening process does the center have for its new employees? What kind of things disqualify someone from being hired?

✓ Are there any entrances to the center that someone could sneak into without being seen? (*A Parents Guide: Child Safety in the 90s*, the Better Information Group, 8815 N. 12th Place, Phoenix, AZ 85020.)

CREEPS ON-LINE?

Because of instant access to others, there is a dark side of computers. On-line services make it possible for people, especially computer literate kids, to find themselves in unpleasant, sexually explicit and even dangerous social situations.

Though all on-line services ban bad conduct, parents have to protect kids from potentially disturbing situations. Several of the services, including America On-line, Prodigy and CompuServe have various types of controls that let parents lock their kids out of the on-line zones where trouble is likeliest. Familiarize yourself with these and use them.

The most important areas to keep kids out of are the "chat" sections. Also consider disabling the so-called "instant message," and bar your kids from the Internet altogether since there is no central authority there (*Wall Street Journal*).

11

Believe It Or Not, You Are Santa Claus (The Holidays!)

I'm always promising not to get jammed in by holiday time pressures. But it's always the same thing—I start picking up little presents here and there, and before you know it, there I am again—two weeks before Christmas and hyperventilating! Typically, it's the time of year I'm short on cash anyway because everybody owes me money—and I owe everybody else money—so I have to do some real creative shopping. But the closer it gets to D-Day, I start adding to the list of those I'd better not forget and on and on....

When Christmas cards from my friends with pictures of their kids start pouring in, my photo phobia routine inevitably kicks in. Hurry! It's time for instant photos, instant developing and instant Christmas cards!

NIFTY GIFTIES

When it comes to picking out a gift for a working Mother, give her something she could really use—like a maid for the day. Or, if you prefer a less expensive route, how about making a set of "IOU" coupons, such as a night of baby-sitting, a sleep over, a play date, a ride home from school or a drink when you need it most, etc.

BEARING IT

If you don't even have time to shop or make something, mail-order companies are great time-savers. The Vermont Teddy Bear Company in Shelburne, Vt., offers beautiful, hand-crafted teddy bear grams. You can order a personalized teddy bear, complete with chocolate truffles, for any occasion. There are birthday and anniversary bears, get well bears, pregnancy and new baby bears, tooth fairy bears and, even, occupation bears—business bears, doctor and nurse bears and teacher bears. To order, call 800-829-BEAR.

FLOWERS FOR HER

Thank goodness for flowers, they can really get you off the hook in a hurry. But who has the spare time to grow the flowers to give as the gifts you didn't have time to go out and get in the first place? But then, who needs a garden? Just pick up the phone and order plants and floral products or arrangements from 800-FLOWERS.

For specialty floral gifts such as gift baskets, gourmet chocolates, fresh fruit and more, call 800-GIFT HOUSE, a division of 800-FLOWERS. Both companies can be reached 24 hours a day, 365 days a year.

FRUITY, NUTTY ... INCLINATIONS

Harry and David, a mail-order company in Medford, OR., offers a variety of home-grown fruits and nuts, home-made cakes and chocolates and meats and cheeses, uniquely packaged in a hand-woven gift basket. They offer a full money back guarantee if you are not satisfied with their products or if the package was delayed. To order, call 800-547-3033.

CALL AVON

For real variety, Avon Products offers everything from makeup to bath products, clothing to fragrances, jewelry to videocassettes, compact discs and cassettes to educational gifts and toys. My favorites—Tranquil Moment's Collection of Aromatherapy bubble bath and creams is a great stress reducer (besides being the perfect scent)! Another favorite is Avon's Anew line of skin care products—I have received countless compliments on my skin after using them. Another great choice is Perfect Wear lipstick—the kind that really stays on your lips—not your coffee cup or your significant other's face. For your nearest Avon representative, call 800-FOR-AVON.

OH, VICTORIA!

From Victoria's Secret, choose anything! Most of us cruise through admiring everything, while despising all the girls in the catalog. For goodness sakes, buy something!

BOOK IT!

Books, too, make great gifts. Whether your friends' taste is romance, mystery, great literature or self-help, most of us have found companionship in books. In fact, if you'd like to give my book as a gift, or for another MasterMedia Limited book, call 800-334-8232 or fax 717-348-9297 and say "Debbie sent me," and receive a $2 discount on the book of your choice. (See the back of the book for a list of MasterMedia books.)

HOLIDAYS WITH THE NEWLY BROKEN FAMILY

Well, here I am, exactly where I never thought I'd be—standing in the center of a broken home. It's fine most days of the year, but not at the holidays.

There isn't a holiday that doesn't cause me agida when we have to decide who is going to be with whom on what holiday. It's the pushes and pulls of "my mother," "her father," "his sisters," and so on. You can never please everybody, and the kids are the ones who really get tense.

Kathryn Black, a psychologist who teaches at Purdue University, has suggested the following ways to help kids of divorced families enjoy the holidays:

✓ Avoiding conflict is the best way to create happy holidays for children of divorce.

✓ Each parent should make sure the children have a gift for the other parent. This shows kids that each parent still wants good things for the other parent.

The Holidays!

✓ If you and your ex-partner practice different religions, don't say anything disparaging about the other's beliefs.

✓ Kids usually divide holidays between parents—spending Thanksgiving with one and Christmas or Hanukkah with the other. On days when the kids are with your ex-partner, plan something to do so you won't feel gloomy.

✓ If your ex-partner gives your child a gift you don't like, it's okay to say, "I'd prefer it if you use that toy at the other house, not here."

12

Around The House

I have this little quirk—I use more paper towels than any other human on the face of the earth! When I discover that I've run out, I sink into depression. Then being home is like being in hell because everywhere I turn there's something that needs to be wiped up with, you guessed it, a paper towel.

A WOMAN'S WORK IS NEVER, EVER DONE

You know it—you still do most or all of the housework even though you work just as much as your husband. No fair! And, now it seems you're doing more housework simply because you have a husband.

DEB*news*

Single Moms spend 16 hours a week on housework versus 20 hours for married Moms. This suggests that a husband generates at least four more hours of housework for a wife to do each week (A Boston University study published in *Working Mother* magazine).

HOW TO HARNESS HUBBY'S HELP

According to John Gray, a relationship therapist and author of *Men Are From Mars, Women Are From Venus*, you can teach your husband to help out more with housework if you:

✓ **Ask for help.** While women are good at sensing the needs of others, men aren't. Men need to be asked for support, otherwise they assume they are giving enough.

✓ **Fine tune your requests.** Though it would be easier not to weigh your every word, it pays to do so. Choose your words and tone of voice carefully when asking for assistance. The key is to avoid making your request sound like a demand, because men are more likely to refuse an "order" than a request. Ask for help in the same nonchalant tone you use when asking someone to pass the butter. Also make your requests as succinct as possible. The longer the query, the more likely your husband is to resist.

✓ **Reward him.** When he finishes a chore, express your gratitude with a remark like, "You're so great about helping with the house." If you want to change his behavior, you have to use a strategy, and the strategy here is positive reinforcement.

This is how Judsen Culbreth, editor of *Working Woman* magazine, gets her husband to help with housework:

✓ Let him choose a chore that he feels comfortable with and enjoys and let him handle it from soup to nuts. Don't interfere and tell him how to do the job, just let him do it himself.

✓ Learn to let go. If your husband is doing the job, but you are still feeling the responsibility of the task, do everything in your power to get if off your mind and let him take responsibility for getting the job done properly.

CUT YOUR HOUSEWORK IN HALF

✓ Survey your home. List the jobs to be accomplished and supplies and equipment needed.

✓ Decide which jobs you want to delegate, hire out, or undertake later.

✓ Begin each room with an easy job so you can savor an immediate sense of success.

✓ Dress comfortably. Wear clothes you don't care about soiling. Protect your hands by wearing work gloves.

✓ Eliminate all distractions. Turn on the answering machine, turn off the TV, and play peppy music.

✓ Don't waste time cleaning clutter. Toss it, recycle it or give it away.

✓ Start with the worst rooms first—that usually means the kitchens and the bathrooms.

✓ Walk around the room instead of criss-crossing it to avoid carrying supplies and equipment back and forth (*Family Circle*).

HOME CONTRACTOR NETWORK

If you find you must hire a contractor to do some work in your home you can make use of these two referral services that help take the guesswork out of choosing building contractors. For $25.00 a year, Home Services Alliance refers members in 19 states to pre-screened remodelers. Contractor Network in Philadelphia has been giving free referrals to homeowners in three states (*Wall Street Journal*).

STAIN, STAIN, GO AWAY

✓ Mildew stains—to remove mildew from leather bags or shoes wipe them with a cloth moistened in a solution of 1 cup denatured alcohol and 1 cup of water. Dry carefully in an airy place.

✓ Fruit or berry stains—stretch the garment over a large heat-proof bowl, and pour boiling water over and through the stains. If the stains remain, try bleaching with hydrogen peroxide or chlorine bleach.

✓ Oil stains—use white chalk to remove grease or oil stains. Rub the chalk onto a washable fabric before laundering.

✓ Coffee stains—soak the garment overnight in a large pan of vinegar and water (heavy on the vinegar). Hang the garment in the sun while dripping wet, then launder as usual. If that doesn't work, try one of the commercial coffee pot cleaners.

✓ Chewing gum stains—put the stained garment in a plastic bag and freeze overnight. The gum should scrape off easily. Another method of gum removal is brushing egg whites on the gum stain with a toothbrush. Then launder the garment as usual to loosen the gum.

✓ Ball point ink stains—saturate the spot with commercial hair spray, let dry and launder.

✓ Crayon mark stains—place the stained garment between two sheets of paper toweling. Go over the area with a warm iron, replacing the paper toweling as the crayon wax adheres to the toweling.

✓ Felt tip pen stains—soak the stain with milk, then launder as usual.

✓ Nail polish stains—remove with amyl acetate nail polish remover (not acetone), then launder as usual.

✓ Blood stains—if the stain is on a washable fabric, wash it in cold water (hot water will set the stain) using mild soap, detergent, or hydrogen peroxide (*Hints, Tips and Smart Advice*, a *Family Circle* book).

OY, OIL

To remove an oil stain from concrete, pour a solution of water and a squirt or two of dishwasher detergent onto the stain. Scrub well, then hose down the spot (*Good Housekeeping*).

LOST AND FOUND

After pulling a load of clothes out of the washer, are
you left wondering where's the other sock? Let it go—it's
gone! When a washer is filled beyond capacity (over-
stuffed) the water level rises above the rim of the inner
tub and spills over into the space between the tub and
the outer casing of the machine. Sometimes a very small
garment—such as a sock or a hankie—can travel down
the drain with the water. New washers have a guard that
prevents this (*McCall's*). Somewhere in this world there is
an infinite reservoir of socks that have gone by the way of
such fate.

DEB*tip*

The first thing you should do when you're on
your hands and knees searching for a lost contact lens or a small piece of jewelry around the
house is get up! Go get the vacuum cleaner and
fasten the toe end of an old nylon over the vacuum hose. The suction will attract the item and
the nylon will keep it from going
into the vacuum (*Woman's Day*).

HOME HELPERS

Keeping your home running like a finely tuned engine
usually means doing most things yourself. But there are
times when things break, or you have a billing question,

or your dog chews up the telephone wires. This list is useful for those times when you need help.

A trusty cleaning person (if not on a regular basis, when you feel like treating yourself):

_____

A trusty carpenter:

_____

A trusty plumber:

_____

A trusty electrician:

_____

A trusty handyman:

_____

A trusty gardener:

_____

Pest control:

_____

Utility company:

_____

Meter reader day:

_____

Phone company/repair #:

_____

Cable company:

_____

Home insurance policy # and agent: _____

_____

Landlord: _____

Building management. company: _____

Superintendent: _____

Others: _____

_____

_____

_____

_____

_____

_____

_____

_____

13

❧

Taking Care
of Business

*"I don't think there is a mother in the
world who is 100 percent comfortable
with the choices she has made. Sure, you
are going to feel a little resentful when
you see someone doing what a part of
you longs to do."*

—DANA FRIEDMAN, CO-PRESIDENT OF THE
FAMILIES AND WORK INSTITUTE

More than 62 percent of American Moms with
kids under 18 now hold jobs, the
Department of Labor reports, an astounding
19 percent jump in the past decade. Just as significant is
the growing number of women working at home—10
million according to a federal labor study. They may not
commute or hold full-time jobs, but they understand the
daily struggle of working and raising a family. That's not
to say that we working Mothers don't feel guilty about the
time we spend away from our kids. Of course we do—
especially when we see a neighbor reveling in staying

home, chaperoning school field trips and being there with cookies and milk afterward. By the same token, at-home Moms confide that when they see us heading off in the morning ready to take on the world—or at least look-ing as if we are—they sometimes wish they had the excitement and independence (not to mention the wardrobe) of a career woman. Researcher Dana Friedman calls this feeling the "wince factor" (*Woman's Day*).

DID YOU KNOW ...

✓ Women make up nearly half of the nation's work force, and 99 percent will work for pay sometime during their lives.

✓ A recent study of more than 7,000 individu-als found that women and men who fit the soci-etal definition of attractiveness typically earn an average of 10 percent more than their less-than-lovely counterparts (*Real Beauty* magazine).

✓ During the last 15 years, American women have experienced an average 3.6 year increase in work-life expectancy, while men's work life expectancy has remained basically unchanged, according to the *New Work Life Expectancy Tables* published annually by Louisville-based Vocational Econometrics. This information is particularly significant to women who are involved in personal injury lawsuits and need to show that their lifetime earning capacity has been reduced as a result of their injuries.

SURVEY SAYS ...

The Working Women Count! survey of 250,000 women, conducted by the U.S. Department of Labor, evoked the following responses from women respondents:

> ✓ *We love our jobs—the satisfaction they give us, the money that comes with them and the independence that follows.*

> ✓ *We like our work so much that we continue in the offices and in the factories in spite of the lack of opportunity, the disparity in pay, the dearth of benefits. More important, we continue to punch the time clock in spite of the monumental juggling act we perform daily trying to balance work and family.*

> ✓ *Being a working Woman is just like being working man except for less pay, less power, less opportunity and the higher expectations....*

TO GET WORKING, TRY NETWORKING

A Gallup Survey, commissioned by *Working Woman* magazine and MCI, interviewed 561 executive women. Here's what it found:

✓ Networking efforts helped half of the respondents land a job, 39% make a career change and 37% get a promotion.

✓ When asked to rate the importance of various non-professional qualities in helping women get ahead, almost all women (93%) rated having networking contacts as being important.

✓ A majority (93%) think seeking advice about a professional issue is a good way to network.

✓ The number-one factor that respondents believe has limited their success is having a family and children (19%) followed by lack of education and/or a degree (14%).

✓ The relative importance of non-professional qualities women think are needed for success were rated as follows:

> ✓ Positive personality—99%
> ✓ Integrity—98%
> ✓ Loyalty—97%
> ✓ Being one of the guys—48%
> ✓ Not having kids—29%
> ✓ Playing golf—24%

The Business Women's Network Directory is the first resource to provide leadership names, numbers and in-depth profiles of the top women's business organizations in America. The directory, which is sponsored by NAS-DAQ, MCI and *Working Woman* magazine, is available for $94.95 by calling 800-48-WOMEN.

BROTHER, CAN YOU SPARE ANOTHER 30 CENTS?

In 1994, women working full-time, year-round, earned a little more than 70 cents for every $1 earned by men. That's up from 60 cents in 1964—an increase of one thin dime in three decades. Broken down by race the numbers are even more troubling. African- American women make only 64 cents and Hispanics just 55 cents. Clearly the Equal Pay Act has failed to eliminate gender-based pay gaps.

A major reason is that so-called "women's jobs," such as clerical work, teaching and nursing among others, have historically been undervalued compared to "men's jobs," such as van driving, construction work, meter reading and carpentry.

PLAY FAIR, FAIR PAY

The Fair Pay Act of 1994, introduced by Eleanor Holmes Norton, D-D.C., takes a needed giant step in going beyond the "equal pay" principle established in 1964. The Fair Pay Act prohibits discrimination in pay for work in equivalent jobs—jobs requiring the same levels of skill, complexity, knowledge and working conditions— even if the actual duties are different.

Typically, job seekers or those who fear discrimination can't get the simplest data from employers, such as aggregate earnings information for women and men, or what proportion of each job category is female. The Fair Pay Act requires that employers provide public disclosure of job classifications and pay statistics (*USA Today*).

OUT OF THE LOOP?

If your relationship with your boss has broken down, it's in your best interest to figure out why you've been left out in the cold and do something to change the situation. Here are some tips suggested by business writer Antonia van der Meer to help you improve your communication with your supervisor:

1. Pay attention to your boss' style. If you can't figure it out, try asking the question directly: "How would you like to receive information from me?"

2. Keep it short and clear. If you're making a presentation, be concise. If you're commenting on a situation, get to the point and tell your boss only what he or she needs to know. Most of us tend to be too wordy. Present your case clearly and with confidence.

3. Ask questions but not too many. Supervisors often don't explain things and employees are scared to ask questions. It's important to ask a few good questions. Focus on asking specific questions that will help you do your assignment better.

4. Give some thought to timing. If your boss is rushing to get something done, this is not the time to discuss a long-range project. Think

about what you wish to communicate and
choose a time and setting that fits your message.
Ask for a friendly favor as you walk to the elevator or parking lot. If you have a quick question,
ask it in the lull before lunch.

5. Pay attention to your attitude. Do you complain a lot? Are you defensive when your work is
criticized? Nobody likes working with chronic
complainers, or with people who start arguing
whenever someone disagrees with them.

6. Listen for meaning as well as words. Resist
the urge to make mental counter-arguments
when your boss is talking or you won't hear the
message. One way to verify the meaning is to
paraphrase an idea: "Are you saying that...?"

7. Don't be afraid to tell your supervisor bad
news. If you've made a mistake, it's better for
your supervisor to hear about it from you.
Inform your boss by saying exactly what happened in as few words as possible and suggest a
plan for solving the problem (*Work and Family
Life*).

Lunch Hour Power!

The lunch hour is becoming one of the most valuable
hours of the day for many working mothers who use the
midday break to accomplish everything from breast-feed-

ing to exercising to grocery shopping, according to the April 1995 issue of *Working Mother.*

Here's what some resourceful Moms are doing:

✓ Visiting their children—if you work close to home, this is great .

✓ Dating their husbands—why not? Your child's already with a caregiver or in school. If you wait till the end of the day to talk to your husband, you may be too exhausted to have any quality time alone.

✓ Grocery shopping—keep a small cooler in the car for perishable items.

✓ Exercising—a lunch-time workout can provide a needed burst of energy.

✓ Working—some parents work through their midday breaks in order to leave an hour earlier to spend more time with their families.

GETTING BACK ON THE JOB TRACK?

Formerly Employed Mothers At the Leading Edge (F.E.M.A.L.E.) offers some helpful advice if you're considering going back to work after raising your children:

Resume Tips

✓ Include a section of your community and volunteer activities. Measurable achievements in charitable activities—such as the ability to organize, motivate a group of workers and achieve your objective—are a strong indication of future performance in the workplace.

✓ Don't try to hide the fact that you've been out of the work force for a time to raise your children at home. Clearly list your earlier years of employment and your current years at home with a positive, confident description. Don't embellish routine work with modifiers—it may appear that you're trying to defend your choice to have been home rather than being sure of your decision.

✓ Many women have chosen to further their education during the "at home" years. Your resume should include these courses to illustrate your commitment to improving yourself and keeping your skills fresh.

Interviewing Tips

When going for job interviews, be prepared to respond to direct questions such as:

✓ How have you kept your work skills up-to-date while you've been home?

✓ What child care arrangements have you made?

✓ What happens if your child is sick and cannot go to school? What happens if your sitter is sick and cannot watch your child?

✓ Explain why this is now the time for you to

seek employment. Are your children now in school full-time? Be as sure of your decision to return to work as you were with your choice to be home.

For more job entry or re-entry help or information, call F.E.M.A.L.E. at 708-941-3553.

SURVIVAL TIPS FOR MOMS THAT WORK AT HOME

✓ Many fast food restaurants have indoor and outdoor playgrounds. This is a great place to go when you want to keep the kids occupied while you work. Miscellaneous "to-do" material such as bill paying, addressing envelopes, stuffing, licking and sticking stamps can be taken to the playground and done over a cup of tea while the kids enjoy an hour or so of playtime.

✓ Borrow a few long, classic movies from the library such as *The Wizard of Oz, The Sound of Music,* or *My Fair Lady.* Don't feel guilty about letting the kids watch movies when you have deadlines to meet.

✓ Ask a trusted neighbor with children if she would like to trade a few hours of child care. A little peace and quiet can be as simple as working out a convenient time to exchange kids.

✓ Ask a reliable neighborhood teen to come over two afternoons a week after school and play with the kids for an hour (*Raising Happy Kids on a Reasonable Budget*).

TURN A TOEHOLD INTO A FOOTHOLD

Ways to promote yourself in the business world:

✓ Return all phone calls or make sure someone in your organization returns them. You never know why a person may be calling.

✓ Be visible—go to professional seminars, luncheons, receptions, dinners and other kinds of gatherings. You have to be out there for people to notice you.

✓ Send a follow-up note to people you meet and would like to stay in touch with—say hello, enjoyed meeting you, mention a mutual area of interest or something noteworthy about the encounter and suggest the possibility of getting together in the future (*The Personal Touch, What You Really Need in Today's Fast-Paced Business World,* by Terrie M. Williams).

TELECOMMUTING ...

Approximately 7.6 million Americans work from home part of the time, according to LINK Resources, a New York City-based technology research and consulting firm. At some point, you may decide working from your part of the time might be a feasible situation (and a more convenient way to maintain your juggling act!).

Here are a few ways to convince your boss it's the way to go:

1. Evaluate your responsibilities. Make a list of the things you could do at home and review the list with your boss.

2. Show how your department or company stands to gain. If you can demonstrate that telecommuting will make you a better employee, your boss is more likely to say yes.

3. Anticipate objections and prepare responses. Your boss may be worried that you can't be there for meeting—tell him or her you'll be there at all costs.

4. Think through the details and suggest which days you'd like to work from home. Explain how you'll stay in touch and discuss the equipment you'll need.

5. Put your proposal and your discussions about it with your boss in writing. Follow up your discussion with a proposal that reiterates the points discussed (*Working Mother* magazine).

DEB*quote*
The best deal about working at home
is you don't need a pass key for
the bathroom!

In 1994, *Working Mother* magazine named the 100 best companies for working mothers, based on opportunities for women to advance, support for child care, and family-friendly benefits. Here are the Top 10 in alphabetical order:

AT&T
Barnett Banks
Fel-PRO
Glaxo
John Hancock
IBM
Johnson & Johnson
Lancaster Laboratories
Nations Bank
Xerox

To obtain a list of all 100 companies, call *Working Woman* magazine, 212-551-9500.

ARE YOU AN ENTREPRENEUR?

" Half of U.S. firms may be woman-owned by the year 2000."
—WORKING MOTHER *MAGAZINE*

One out of three women working in corporate America say they would like to leave the rat race behind and start their own business. They would like to have more control over their lives, increase their personal fulfillment, and create more flexibility in their work schedules. However, two of the most common emotional obstacles to starting a business women experience are the thought of giving up a regular paycheck and fear of the unknown. A very tangible obstacle they face is insufficient funds or capital, according to a recent poll sponsored by Avon Products, Inc.

WHAT CAN I DO?

DEB*quote*
When entering a new venture,
do what you know! Go for it!

Do what you love and are good at. If you love parties, organize birthday parties for kids. If you love cooking, begin your own catering service. Start with small groups and gradually work up to larger crowds. You can do everything from food to decorations and clean up.

If you love sewing and are nimble with needles, sew aprons for local restaurants or stores; or start a home tailoring service. Many people can alter hems, shorten sleeves take in waists etc. If you are partial to pets, create a dog walking, bathing or boarding service.

If you are one of those rare human types that actually like to clean things, start a home or office cleaning service. If you're good with numbers, start a bookkeeping service for small organizations. If you like kids and teaching, tutor children who need help with their homework; or begin your own baby-sitting service.

GROUND ZERO—FINANCES

The first thing you have to do when heading off on your own business venture is find out what kind of financing is available. Start with the following potential sources:

✓ Prospective owners
✓ Family and friends
✓ Banks
✓ Commercial finance companies
✓ Venture capital funds
✓ State and federal funding programs
✓ Local development companies

SOURCES OF EXPERT ADVICE

✓ An attorney can help you determine and establish the appropriate organizational structure, and/or legal form for your enterprise. Your attorney will ensure that your business is in compliance with local, state and federal regulations. He or she will evaluate, negotiate, and prepare legal documents, including leases and sales contracts, and deal with legal issues and problems with employees, customers, suppliers and others with whom you have a business relationship.

✓ A certified public accountant can help you set up your bookkeeping system, draw up financial statements, determine cash requirements for each phase of your business. He or she also will prepare tax forms and do general financial planning.

✓ A banker can help you open a business checking account, establish a line of credit, secure a loan, and manage cash flow. He or she will help you make prudent investments and manage both corporate and personal finances.

✓ An insurance agent or broker can help you understand different types of insurance, including: life, medical, auto, disability income, fire, general liability, umbrella liability, business interruption and workmen's compensation. He or she will identify and assess your economic risks and help you arrange for adequate insurance coverage (*Take Control Of Your Life: Start Your Own Business*, an Avon Product's book).

WHEN TO SEEK LEGAL COUNSEL

Daniel A. DeVito of the prestigious New York City law firm Weil, Gotshal and Manges, offers the following great legal advice :

✓ Entering into any type of contract (most transactions that involve the transfer of money can be characterized as a contract)
✓ Investing money
✓ Buying insurance
✓ Dealing with defective merchandise
✓ Purchasing or leasing a car

✓ Finding a place to live
✓ In financial trouble
✓ In need of a will
✓ Having trouble at work
✓ When you think you've got a good idea.

FINDING A LAWYER

✓ If you were previously represented by an attorney and were satisfied with the relationship but that attorney doesn't have the expertise you currently need, ask him or her to recommend someone with the necessary experience.

✓ Ask a family member or friend who is an attorney for a recommendation.

✓ Ask your employer to recommend an attorney—if you feel comfortable letting your employer know that you need legal assistance.

✓ Contact a your state or local bar association.

✓ Consult a legal directory—such as the Martindale-Hubbell directory—to find the names and firm affiliations of attorneys throughout the country, categorized by geographical location and practice area.

HOW TO NEGOTIATE EFFECTIVELY

Effective negotiation requires that you know the relevant facts and understand your available options and that you let the other side know that you're knowledgeable about the subject being negotiated.

Confidence is perhaps the most important weapon in negotiating, but confidence is not the same as being fool-hardy. Negotiation means giving something to get some-thing in return. In order to get what you want, you must first identify what it is you are willing to give up. Prioritize you goals—make a list of those items you absolutely must have, those you would like to have but could live without, and those that you are willing to give up. Once you do this, try to imagine and understand the other side's pri-orities.

While negotiating, it may not be in your best interest to emphasize the items important to you in a way that reveals your priorities to the other side. In some cases, if they know what you really want they will try to take as much as possible from you before you get it. In other instances, it may be more prudent to let the other side know from the outset that certain things are simply not negotiable.

The bottom line in negotiating is to be reasonable, remain calm and try to feel out the other side.

THE OFFICE OF WOMEN'S BUSINESS OWNERSHIP

Women are starting new businesses at twice the rate of men. By the year 2000, it is expected that 40 percent of all small businesses will be owned by women. The Office of Women's Business Ownership focuses on the needs of the increasing number of women business owners.

Established in 1979 to design and implement a nation-al policy to support women entrepreneurs, the organization offers a wide range of services and resources through a national network of local Small Business Administration offices. Potential and established women business owners will find many programs designed to promote and market women business owners, including:

✓ The Women's Network for Entrepreneurial Training, which is a one-year mentor relationship between successful women entrepreneurs and other women-owned businesses that are ready to take a growth step.

✓ Training conferences on how to gain access to credit, including information on the Small Business Administration's guaranteed lending programs such as the Small Loan Incentive and Microlending.

✓ Conferences on how to sell products and services to the Federal government (procurement).

✓ Demonstration Project program, which was authorized by The Women's Business Ownership Act of 1988 to establish long-term training and counseling centers for women around the country (The U.S. Small Business Administration, Washington, D.C.).

GOTTA GO!

As you might have guessed, I've gotta run. I hope you enjoyed the book, and that it will be of some help to you while juggling all of your busy routines. Before I go, let me leave you with an excerpt from my Working Woman's Yap song—'cause women don't rap, they YAP!

... From early in the morning
'Til we pass out late at night
We're all living legends of
The working woman's plight
A zillion, million things to do,
And always in a hurry!
Phone calls in a flurry!
It's no wonder that we worry!

Chorus:

This is your life!
You REALLY, REALLY, REALLY need a wife!
Can't take much more of that old stress and strife
And nothing personal honey,
But please NOT TONIGHT!...

To purchase an audio cassette of the entire Working Woman's Yap song, send $5.00 to:

Debbie Nigro
P.O. Box 4005
Grand Central Station
New York, NY 10163

WORKING MOM ON THE RUN

ABOUT THE AUTHOR

Debbie Nigro hosts a two-hour nationally syndicated radio talk show "The Working Mom On the Run (A.K.A. What The Heck Happened To My Life?," as well as weekday vignettes. Her career to date has spanned 16 years in broadcasting, holding positions ranging from radio news reporter to television host and producer. She owns Sweet Talk Productions, and has produced an exercise video in conjunction with Avon Products, Inc.

As a perfect counterbalance to her hectic days, Debbie lives in New Rochelle, N.Y., with Alexis, her seven-year-old daughter.

Additional copies of *The Working Mom on The Run Manual* may be ordered by sending a check for $9.95 (please add $2.00 for postage and handling for the first copy and $1.00 for each additional copy) to:

MasterMedia Limited
17 East 89th Street
New York, NY 10128
(800) 334-8232
(212) 260-5600
(212) 546-7638 (fax)

Debbie is available as a key-note speaker and comedian. Please contact MasterMedia's Speakers' Bureau for availability and fee arrangements. Call Tony Colao at (908) 359-1612; fax: (908) 359-1647.

MASTERMEDIA BACK LIST

Other MasterMedia Child Care & Parenting Books

To order MasterMedia books, either visit your local bookstore or call 1-800-334-8232.

THE PREGNANCY AND MOTHERHOOD DIARY: Planning the First Year of Your Second Career, by Susan Schiffer Stautberg, is the first and only undated appointment diary that shows how to manage pregnancy and career. ($12.95 spiral-bound)

AGING PARENTS AND YOU: A Complete Handbook to Help You Help Your Elders Maintain a Healthy, Productive and Independent Life, by Eugenia Anderson-Ellis, is a complete guide to providing care to aging relatives. It gives practical advice and resources to the adults who are helping their elders lead productive and independent lives. Revised and updated. ($9.95 paper)

MANAGING IT ALL: Time-Saving Ideas for Career, Family, Relationships and Self, by Beverly Benz Treuille and Susan Schiffer Stautberg, is written for women who are juggling careers and families. Over two hundred career women (ranging from a TV anchorwoman to an investment banker) were interviewed. The book contains many humorous anecdotes on saving time and improving the quality of life for self and family. ($9.95 paper)

BREATHING SPACE: Living and Working at a Comfortable Pace in a Sped-Up Society, by Jeff Davidson, helps readers to handle information and activity overload, and gain greater control over their lives. ($10.95 paper)

BALANCING ACTS! Juggling Love, Work, Family and Recreation, by Susan Schiffer Stautberg and Marcia Worthing, provides strategies to achieve a balanced life by reordering priorities and setting realistic goals. ($12.95 paper)

MANAGING YOUR CHILD'S DIABETES, by Robert Wood Johnson IV, Sale Johnson, Casey Johnson, and Susan Kleinman, brings help to families trying to understand diabetes and control its effects. ($10.95 paper)

WOMEN INCORPORATED is a national organization dedicated to helping women entrepreneurs in their ventures. While WI's major goal is to provide women entrepreneurs increased access to capital, WI helps its members by introducing discounts on products and services usually available only to larger companies and strengthening the national voice of women business owners.

As a member of Women Incorporated you will be eligible for access to our **$150 million loan fund** earmarked especially for WI members, secured and unsecured credit cards, and health insurance even if you are self-employed. You will also receive informational materials to guide you in running your business, and WI's national quarterly magazine.

Membership Benefits include discounts on products and services from companies such as:

- AT&T
- IBM
- Federal Express
- Northwest Airlines
- USAir
- Sam's Club
- Penny Wise Office Products
- Health Insurance
- Credit Cards
- Printing
- And Many More!

For more information on WOMEN INCORPORATED please fill in and return the attached card.

FROM:

Name

Name of Company

Address

City   State   Zip

Phone (   )   Fax (   )

TO:
Membership Coordinator
WOMEN INCORPORATED
1401 21st Street, Suite 310
Sacramento, CA 95814